Hiking in North Florida with William Bartram

25 Hikes

Volume One

Also by G. Kent

Nonfiction

*Running with Razors and Soul:
A Handbook for Competitive Runners*

Fiction

Bandits on the Rim

Grinners

Granada Hills Blood

Hiking in North Florida with William Bartram

25 Hikes

Volume One

G. Kent

Bandit Press

© Copyright 2014 by Gary R. Kent

All rights reserved. No part of this book may be used or reproduced by any means, graphic, electronic or mechanical, including photocopying, recording, taping or by any information storage retrieval system without the written permission of the publisher except in the case of brief quotations embodied in critical articles or reviews.

ISBN – 13: 9780692289723
ISBN – 10: 0692289720
LCCN: 2014-916980

Bandit Press
2329 NE 8th Place
Ocala, Fl 34470
kentib@earthlink.net

This book may be ordered from the publisher, through booksellers at Barnes and Noble, or online at createspace.com or amazon.com.

CONTENTS

Dedication	viii
Foreword by Todd Carstenn	xi
Introduction	1
Prologue – Hiking With Adults	3
Seasons	4
Wildlife and Insects	7
What To Carry	10
Rain and Lightening	12
Uphill and Downhill	14
Hunting	15
Firearms	17
Lost	19
Rangers	21
Leave It Alone	23
Nature by Henry David Thoreau	24

Hike # 1 – Ocklawaha Prairie — 25

Hike # 2 – Salt Springs River Trail — 30

Hike # 3 – Land Bridge Trail — 33

Hike # 4 – Lake Eaton and Sinkhole Trail — 37

Hike # 5 – Chornobyl Memorial Forest — 41

Hike # 6 – Sunnyhill Restoration Area — 45

Hike # 7 – Marshall Swamp — 49

Hike # 8 – St. George Island State Park – Gap Point Trail — 52

Hike # 9 – Tate's Hell – High Bluff Coastal Trail — 56

Hike # 10 – St. Joseph Peninsula State Park – Peninsula Trail — 59

Hike # 11 – Paynes Prairie State Park – Bolen Bluff Trail — 63

Hike # 12 – Paynes Prairie State Park – Cone Dike Trail — 67

Hike # 13 – Paynes Prairie State Park – Chacala Pond Trail — 71

Hike # 14 – Barr Hammock — 74

Hike # 15 – Pat's Island — 77

Hike # 16 – The Yearling Trail   81

Hike # 17 – Silver Springs State Park –   85
            River Trail

Hike # 18 – Silver Springs State Park –   88
            Swamp Trail

Hike # 19 – Silver Springs   91
            Conservation Area

Hike # 20 – Woody's Trail   95

Hike # 21 – Pruitt Trail   99

Hike # 22 – Sawgrass Island State Preserve   103

Hike # 23 – Zay Prairie   106

Hike # 24 – Horseshoe Lake   109

Hike # 25 – East Grove Trail   112

Epilogue – We Have To Care   115

Happy Trails   116

A Clear Midnight by Walt Whitman   117

Recommended Reading

Acknowledgments

About the Author

Dedication

"Having contemplated this admirable grove, I proceeded toward the shrubberies on the banks of the river, and though it was now late December, the aromatic groves appeared in full aroma."
—William Bartram, 1774

In 1773, William Bartram embarked on a four-year journey through eight Southern states. By 1774 he reached North Florida, which was briefly held by the British, and visited a Seminole Indian village at Cuscowilla. When Bartram explained his mission to Ahaya, chief of the Alachua band of Seminole, the bemused chief began calling him Puc-pugee, the flower hunter.

Indeed, William Bartram took notes and made drawings of much of the local flora and fauna. He experienced North Florida long before it became a U.S. Territory or State.

William Bartram's 1791 *Travels* is an American classic that describes North Florida as an exotic and sub-tropical region of incomparable beauty. Readers' imaginations were captured by descriptions of roaring alligators, giant rattlesnakes, and lush and tropical landscapes.

During Bartram's trip:

- Seminole children saluted him with cheerfulness.

- He described some of his hikes as "harsh treatment from thorny thickets and prickly vines."

- He reported natural orange groves in full fragrant bloom.

- He crossed the River Styx near Cross Creek, later the home of Pulitzer Prize winning author Marjorie Kinnan Rawlings.

- He explored the Alachua Savannah, or what is known today as Paynes Prairie, near the University town of Gainesville.

- He camped near Silver Glen Springs where at night wolves made off with fish that were hanging directly above his sleeping head.

- He experienced a North Florida that hikers today can only dream about and imagine.

The Florida State Parks motto is "The Real Florida." In 1774, William Bartram witnessed and experienced "The Real Florida" and the natural condition of the environment. Our vision and quest should be to preserve and protect as much of "The Real Florida" as possible for the enjoyment of present-day and future generations. Although he lived and died in Philadelphia, North Floridians consider Bartram to be an honorary citizen of our state.

This book is dedicated to the vision and memory of William Bartram (1739-1823).

Foreword

"My most memorable hikes can be classified as 'shortcuts that backfired.'"
—Edward Abbey

    A hiker who's a writer and a writer who's a hiker. Who better to pen a book about hikes through the trails, forests, conservation areas and wilds of this area in North Florida that we call home. And home is what these trails are to Gary Kent. You see, a problem I've encountered with other books similar to this one, where some outdoor "expert" tells us what to do and see, is that they seem distant. Or that they might be trying to show off a bit about how much they know that we don't. That's not the case here. Gary Kent treats these areas like his home, his own changing and sometime dangerous and cacophonous backyard.
    During the description of almost every hike, he tells us to "take care to" notice a spur trail which meanders off to a view that otherwise might be missed, or to "take care to" listen to the breeze sing through the pines. For some writers, this "take care to" admonition might be a throwaway line. But Gary means it, in two ways. Of course he means, "Hey guys, you don't want to miss this, Nature at her finest." But he also emphasizes, without capitals, the CARE part. His admonition now means that we must nurture, hold dear

and cherish. We must not only take care TO, but we must take care OF these trails, and all of God's gifts, included in, on, around and above them. He agrees with Edward Abbey that now more than ever our environment needs defenders. And of course good hikers and campers make staunch defenders.

Speaking of Edward Abbey, Gary introduced me to *The Monkey Wrench Gang* many years ago, and what struck me most about Cactus Ed was his passion, his enthusiasm for all things outdoors. It is because of this contagious energy and willingness to stand up to would-be polluters of Mother Earth that I've read every one of Abbey's books, fiction and non-fiction alike.

When I read, I want to know, I want to feel it in my gut, that what the writer is saying MATTERS to him. That's why I love Gary Kent's books so much, and that's why this hiking book works for me. Every pine tree, every pinecone, every spur trail. The sinkholes and gentle rises. The cisterns and grass berms. The screech of the hawk and the solemn silence of the vulture hundreds of feet above. All of it matters to Gary and it comes through in this book.

When I first met Gary, 33 years ago, I wasn't a hiker or camper. Now I'm both, and more. The reason I say "more" is that I believe when we hike and camp we simply do become more—more a part of something vast, more than merely ourselves. We're out in a stand of pines, alone and listening and feeling how small we are in the scope of things, and yet we're not alone and we're not small. We're more. In this book, Gary offers us 25 ways to feel that.

I'll end my part of this with one of my favorite Edward Abbey quotes.

"There are some good things to be said about walking. Not many, but some. Walking takes longer…thus it stretches time and prolongs life. Walking makes the world much bigger and thus more interesting. The Utopian technologists foresee a future for us in which distance is annihilated. To be everywhere at once is to be nowhere forever, if you ask me."

And so the hiker who's a writer and the writer who's a hiker takes us along on these 25 journeys. Put your boots on, pack your dog-eared copy of *Walden* or *Desert Solitaire*, and you're off. See you on the trail.

Todd Carstenn
Ocala, Florida

Introduction

"There's more to life than hiking... but not much more."
—Fis Robin

There seems to be a consensus among outdoor types that Utah is the most diverse and beautiful state in America. I hear it all the time. Yep, I've been there, and it is nice, but I vigorously disagree. In its own unique style, Florida is just as beautiful as Utah, or any other western state, and North Florida is the heart of the matter.

North Florida has crystal clear springs, lakes and rivers, as well as pristine wetlands, spacious prairies and sub-tropical swamps. It has ancient groves of oak and cypress along with vast swaths of slash, longleaf, loblolly and sand pine. Soothing trade winds scatter the clouds and fragrant scents across the peninsula with a hint of Atlantic or Gulf of Mexico spray. The wildlife is exquisite.

True, Utah has the mountains, but where are its beaches?

The 25 hikes in this book are mostly two to four miles in length. On some trails you can hike farther if you choose. These trails should be hiked at a leisurely pace in order to be experienced and enjoyed. After all, life is not always a workout.

There's the first trail marker up ahead. Lace your hiking boots and load the daypack. North Florida is ready to sparkle.

Prologue – Hiking With Adults

"What's with all these drinkers with hiking problems?"
—Bearpaw 88

I love kids. There, I said it. I was even a kid once. The prologue's sub-title, Hiking with Adults, does not imply kids are never welcome on a hike. It means there are times when adults need to be alone, or with adult company, without the responsibilities and restraints of a gang of little tykes hanging onto a leg.

Unfortunately, the presence of children on a trail can hinder adult thought, adult conversation and adult activity. Some of those adult activities might include an adult beverage and a blanket for adult shenanigans.

Adults require and deserve the right of decompression from their daily stressful lives. What better place to relax than in the North Florida wilderness?

Seasons

"There's no such thing as bad weather, only unsuitable clothing."
—Alfred Wainwright

There are really only two seasons in North Florida—summer and a little cooler. Actually, November through March can average in the fifties, but it's certainly not the type of cold endured in Montana or Minnesota. Yes, North Florida can be gross in the summer, but when Buffalo, New York is buried under fifteen-foot snowdrifts, the clear skies and fifty-two degree temperatures in North Florida transform the area into a wilderness paradise for hikers, backpackers, campers, kayakers, mountain bikers and horse riders. Winter Wonderland, I call it.

My strong recommendation is to stay home from June through September. Summer in North Florida is hot and humid. It is also the bug and hurricane season.

My parents, bless them both, lived in Los Angeles and were truly baffled by my move to North Florida. The mosquitoes and humidity, they howled. Then one Christmas my Dad and I had this phone conversation:

"Your mother and I are planning a visit," Dad said.

"Great," I replied. "I'll show you some nice places."

"We got a super-saver deal on a two-bedroom timeshare. I used my Marriott points."

"Where's the condo?" I asked. Mom loved the water so my guess was Ormond or Crescent Beach."

"Buena Vista."

"Buena Vista? Buena Vista is Disney World."

"We can see Epcot from the balcony."

"Dad," I said, "you don't even like Disney World. Mom loves the ocean."

"We got a super-saver deal," he repeated.

I became exasperated. "Okay, fine. When are you coming to Buena Vista?"

"August."

"August?" I wailed. "You're going to hate August. The mosquitoes and humidity."

"We got a super-saver deal."

Please, don't think you can tough it on the trail during a North Florida summer. You can't. The springs, lakes, beaches and even Disney World are tolerable because of the water and distractions, but hiking on a North Florida trail during the summer will feel like the Inquisition of Humidity and Bug Bites has ensnared you. Trust me, it's worse than you imagine. You will sweat walking from your air-conditioned motel to your air-conditioned car. Not just a little dampness either.

You'll sweat right through your clothes. After jogging in the summer, I look as though someone pushed me in a pool.

Come to North Florida from November to March. It's a Winter Wonderland.

Wildlife and Insects

"In Georgia and South Carolina, there had been plenty of mosquitoes, but in Florida, they had reinforcements."
—Jennifer Pharr Davis

North Florida has nearly every mammal, reptile and bird known to North America. Far too many to list. We have the marquee stars: bear, panther, bobcat, fox, deer, coyote, otter, manatee and alligator. A few of these animals can be threatening, but there is one simple rule to follow and, if you follow it, you will never be in danger from animals. Leave them alone, period. Don't mess with them. Look and enjoy, but stay back. No matter how cute, cuddly or friendly they may appear they are still wild animals.

Never feed an animal. Never approach an animal. Do not attempt to get up close for a photo. No selfies with an alligator.

This advice applies to snakes as well. North Florida has four poisonous species: rattlesnake, copperhead, coral, and moccasin or cottonmouth. Don't try to pick one up. Remember, snakes want nothing to do with you and, given the opportunity, they will almost always try to escape. The biggest snake danger is to stumble upon one by accident. Watch where you put your feet, especially around brush and swampy water.

Contrary to popular opinion, snakes are not aggressive. They are still more afraid of you than you of them. I've stepped on two rattlesnakes without getting bit or even eliciting a rattle. Snake aggression is measured by how close you can get to them before they feel alarmed. The distance for rattlesnakes is two to three feet, and they will rattle long before you get that close. At four to five feet, cottonmouths have the least amount of tolerance among North Florida's poisonous snakes. They can be angry little suckers, but even a cottonmouth won't start the fight. All other snakes in North Florida are harmless and important to the environment, not to mention beautiful. Plus, in the winter most of our snakes are inactive.

We have bears, but no grizzlies. Stand your ground and make yourself appear bigger. Make noise. Do not run. Bears like to chase things and they can outrun you. Same goes for a panther. However, if you see a panther, my advice is to play the lottery that week because you will win.

Don't worry about gators because none of the hikes in this book go into the water. If a gator is sunning itself on land, leave it alone. Back off.

A few species that may surprise you are wild horses, bison and monkeys. The horses were brought by Spanish explorers and herded by the Seminole. Bison were reintroduced to Paynes Prairie from Oklahoma in the 1970s. And rhesus monkeys were covertly released along the Silver River in 1938 by a would-be P. T. Barnum.

Florida birding is incredible. I'm no expert, but I see them everywhere. North Florida is home to bald eagle, osprey, nearly every kind of hawk and owl, turkey vulture and what I refer to as ACEHI (anhinga, crane, egret, heron and ibis.) Plus, tons of little guys. Our state bird is the feisty mockingbird, while a personal favorite of mine is the swallowtail kite.

Insects. Bugs. North Florida has every kind of biting and stinging pest known to humankind. Many can be fierce and tenacious. The mosquito has the big rep, but my personal enemies are the horsefly, no-see-um and fire ant. The good news is that North Florida insects are pretty tame in the winter. I still carry spray at all times. In fact, it's a good idea to always spray your boots, socks and cuffs to discourage ticks, chiggers and brown recluse spiders.

This word to the wise should be sufficient. Every year there are people whose vacations or weekend outings end unhappily because of their own foolishness or carelessness. Follow the advice in this chapter, use common sense, and have a great time hiking. Don't become a statistic.

What to Carry

"May the forest be with you."
—Obi Wan the Hiker

Every publication has its special list of what to carry on a day hike. My list is ordinary and certainly not complete. One item I recommend that most lists don't mention is a lightweight chair. Any aluminum frame or fold up contraption will work. This may sound burdensome, but when you're ready to relax on the trail a chair is sweet.

Also:
Hat
Sunglasses
Sunscreen
Bug spray
Raingear
Flashlight
Matches or Lighter
Newspaper (to help start a fire)
Snacks
Water
Book or Magazine
Knife
Extra T-Shirt
Extra Socks

Extra Fleece or Sweatshirt
Whistle

The extra T-shirt is for the sweat on the hike out. If it's cold, a wet T-Shirt can be miserable. Extra socks are in case you stumble into muck or water. Now for the secret stuff. A blanket or sheet is great for naps or…sex. Yes, I said sex. If the weather cooperates, sex in the wild can be magical. Also, bring along your favorite adult beverage. Whether it is beer, spirits or fine wine, an adult beverage on the trail can always help with decompression. You want it cold? There are excellent small collapsible coolers for sale, or try my little trick. Take a one-gallon zip lock bag and put in ice along with your beer or wine, or use the ice for mixed drinks. The bag may leak slightly, but it's well worth the effort.

Rain and Lightning

"I don't think that storm is heading our way."
—Hammock Hangar

Allow me to re-emphasize—when in North Florida, bring raingear. It doesn't matter if the state is in a two-year drought, or if it's sunny and clear and the weather channel reports 0% chance of precipitation. Bring raingear. This is North Florida, and a storm can blow in from the Gulf or the Atlantic at a moment's notice. I'd rather have the raingear and it be sunny, than not have it and suffer a downpour.

Any questions?

Lightning. North Florida is the lightning capital of the world. Up close and personal, the flash and boom of lightning and thunder can be horrific. If you hear the sound of thunder, you could be in danger. If a boom quickly follows the flash, you could be in REAL danger.

Seek a low place such as a valley, ravine or any depression. Take shelter under a thick grove of small trees. Stay away from the big trees because they can act as lightning rods. Squat low to the ground on the balls of your feet. Stand on your pack and put your raingear over your head. Place your hands over your ears and head between your knees. Make yourself the smallest target possible and minimize contact with the ground. DO NOT LIE FLAT ON THE GROUND! Remember: stay calm. Take all precautions. You're not going to be struck by the lightning. The odds are way in your favor. Sure, it happens, but a tire from a Southwest jet could also fall and hit you on the head.

Uphill and Downhill

"The next section is all downhill."
—Bearpaw 88

Uphill and downhill do not enter the equation in North Florida.

Hunting

"This wasn't in the brochure."
—Slogger

Beware: hunting season in North Florida is November to mid-January. Fortunately, only four hikes in this book traverse areas that allow hunting. Nevertheless, it would be wise to know the boundaries of hunting areas and keep your eyes open.

I will not impugn all hunters. The vast majorities are extraordinarily experienced, conscientious, responsible and skilled. Although I'll never relate to the thrill of shooting a deer in the head from a tree stand, I do understand that hunting is part of the American heritage and I defend the right to hunt. In fact, many hunting organizations, such as Ducks Unlimited, are champions of wetland and forest preservation.

There is, however, a different breed of hunter. When I first moved to the Ocala National Forest, I witnessed hunters standing on the cabs of their pickup trucks with a rifle in one hand and bottle of Jim Beam in the other. Hunters who use packs of dogs, saltlicks, CB's, ATV's or any other type of vehicle to trap or chase down their quarry are cowards. Show me a hunter who dresses in camo, paints his face, and crawls into the woods with a rifle or bow, and that will be a hunter who has earned my respect.

Also, in North Florida, a hunter must identify a deer as a buck before firing a shot. Wouldn't it also be wise to have all members of your party accountable before blasting away? How then is it possible to accidentally shoot Uncle Ned or cousin Zeke, who are probably wearing orange vests and certainly don't look like deer? Yet shooting accidents take place every year.

It's probably a smart idea to stay out of the Ocala National Forest during hunting season.

Firearms

"I don't have to outrun the bear...
I only have to outrun you."
   —Toddrick C.

I do not carry a firearm into the woods, though maybe I should. Judge Hale Stancil told me during a Marion County-sponsored gun class, "I'd never go into the Ocala National Forest unarmed."

If I did carry a firearm, it would be a small .38 or .380, and I'd be very careful about whom I told. I wouldn't carry a firearm out of fear of the wildlife. Animals run away. Plus, if you shot a bear, you'd probably only piss him off.

No, if I did carry a firearm, it would be for people. Unfortunately, wilderness does attract its share of crazies. After all, North Florida was the stomping grounds of Bundy, Rolling and Wuornos, and each of them used the woods at times during their murder sprees. Bad things have recently happened at the Hopkins Prairie and Hidden Pond areas of the Ocala National Forest. When newspapers report that the crime rate is rising on the Appalachian Trail, the granddaddy of the U.S. trail system, hikers have reason to take notice.

Granted, if a bullet came from a distance, or a bad person approached in a friendly manner, a firearm in my daypack would probably be ineffective. But, given the slightest warning, a firearm could help put up a spirited struggle.

However, I believe carrying a firearm is not worth the trouble. Statistics show that I'm far more likely to shoot a friend or myself than an evildoer. If you disagree, I respect that. There's no need for paranoia on the trail. Be practical around strangers and stay alert.

Lost

"My grandmother started walking five miles a day when she was 90. She's 93 today, and we don't know where the hell she is."
—Ellen DeGeneres

I've always boasted I cannot get lost. I've bushwhacked through thick forests and swamps, and even tried to get lost to no avail. Twice, however, I took a wrong turn and ended up miles away from my truck. That'll certainly take the wind out of your sails.

Bushwhacking, hiking on an unmarked trail or missing a turn can put you in the wrong place and lead to confusion. Few people get lost while staying on the trail. Usually, if you get disoriented you merely turn around.

One time, my wife Elaine and I hiked a non-maintained trail in Yellowstone National Park. It probably wasn't a good idea. I'm sure the trail was non-maintained for a good reason, probably grizzly bear activity. But we discovered the orange blazes on the trees and took off following them. After relaxing for a few hours at a gorgeous meadow, we started our hike back to the car with Elaine in the lead. Within an hour, she stopped suddenly and said, "I don't see any orange blazes." I looked up and quickly realized we had wandered off the scant path. Now we were lost in the

Yellowstone wilderness. I took off my pack and backtracked. After a quarter of a mile, I spotted an orange blaze. I hung my coat on a tree and went back for Elaine.

    The point is, situations like that can happen to anyone at any time.

    Tell someone where you are going and when you should be back. I might add that you shouldn't hike alone, but that would be the height of hypocrisy since over 75% of my hikes are solo. I'm a big advocate of solo hiking because the experience is more personal and intense.

    If you get lost or turned around, don't panic. You're not going to die. Never leave the trail. There is no such thing as a shortcut when you are lost. Try to return the way you came. If you get frustrated, sit down and rest. Drink some water and think. Scan the area for landmarks. Eat a snack and blow your whistle. If it starts to get dark, stay put and prepare to spend the night. Make yourself as comfortable and sheltered as possible. Signal with your flashlight and build a fire. Wait until morning to try to establish your bearings. Remember that even the most experienced hikers sometimes run into problems. As the great frontiersman Daniel Boone once said, "I've never been lost, but I was mighty turned around for three days once."

    If you spend a night out in the woods, I guarantee the cavalry will be out in full force in the morning.

Rangers

"Rangers who don't range have a tendency to become assholes."
—Grinners

    I have a love/hate relationship with rangers. Most are helpful and friendly, and they are genuine lovers and protectors of the parks and preserves we all love and enjoy. Also, I concede, there is a huge population of ignorant people that the rangers, not me, must deal with. That said, some of the most intolerant, jack-booted thugs in the forest are rangers. Their I-know-it-all and I'm-the-boss attitudes can be officious, obnoxious and petty.

    I have had rangers:

- Shriek at me because my campfire was five inches outside the grate during a downpour.

- Shake their fists at me because my entrance pass was on the dash instead of taped to the windshield.

- Beat their chest and demand that I remove my backpacking tent from a spacious tent pad because there were already two other small backpacking tents on the site.

- Expose their fangs and screech at me to obey trail restrictions *before* I got on the trail.

- Threaten me with a $75 fine for leaving a water cup unattended on a picnic table.

    Still, I have met fine rangers, and they are the front-line defenders of the American environment. They serve in the trenches of the environmental wars and deserve our respect. In fact, their jobs become increasingly difficult and stressful each year because funding is abysmal and Federal and State governments don't seem to care.

    William Bartram would not be happy.

Leave It Alone

"When I found the skull in the woods, the first thing I did was call the police. But then I got curious about it. I picked it up, and started wondering who this person was, and why he had deer horns."
—Jack Handy

"Please! Do not drop your cigarette butts on the ground. The fish crawl out at night to smoke them, and we are trying to get them to quit."
—Everglades National Park

Please do not deface or take any natural feature or historical artifact from any of our parks or preserves.

Please do not litter. It's like a spit in the face to America.

Leave only footprints, take only photos and memories.

Nature

O nature! I do not aspire
To be the highest in thy choir, -
To be a meteor in thy sky,
Or comet that may rage on high;
Only a zephyr that may blow
Among the reeds by the river low;
Give me thy most privy place
Where to run my airy race.

In some withdrawn, unpublic mead
Let me sigh upon a reed,
Or in the woods, with leafy din,
Whisper the still evening in:
Some still work give me to do, -
Only – be it near to you!

For I'd rather be thy child
And pupil, in the forest wild,
Than be the king of me elsewhere,
And most sovereign slave of care;
To have one moment of thy dawn,
Than share the city's year forlorn.

Henry David Thoreau

Hike # 1

Ocklawaha Prairie

*"You're off to great places,
Today is your day,
Your forest is waiting,
So...get on your way."*
—Dr. Suess

Directions – From Ocala head east on SR 40 for 12 miles. At Four Corners, turn right (south) on CR 314A. Follow road for 7 miles, and turn right on 137th Avenue Road. Go 0.8 miles west to parking lot. Watch for signs.

Ocklawaha Prairie is a gem of a hike. In North Florida, a prairie is an expansive wet marsh. This prairie is vast. Hike as little as 2 miles roundtrip, or 9 miles on the loop. My recommendation is to hike out 0.8 miles and cross the Ocklawaha River via the small bridge.

From the parking lot, follow the diamond-shaped trail markers along an old muck farm road. As you hike west, check out the fairly young longleaf pine forest to the south. With the aid of the Forest Service, longleaf pines are slowly making a comeback in North Florida. After about 0.5 miles, make a sweeping left in front of a large open meadow, and drop down to the Ocklawaha River.

Cross the bridge. On the other side is a covered observation platform with magnificent views. After taking a break, hike the well-built boardwalk that will drop you smack dab in the middle of the prairie. The 360-degree views are stunning, and the sky is bigger than Montana.

Sit on the railing at the end of the boardwalk and watch the sunset. Then hike out with a flashlight.

The first time I took this trail, the bridge over the Ocklawaha River was being reconstructed. There were no wooden planks, only thin metal beams. I was forced to inch my way across on a twelve-inch-wide beam while gripping onto the connecting spans. Halfway across I was twenty-five feet above the river, and the connecting beams were out of my reach for about six feet. I tightroped to the next crossbeam. What really concerned me was that I had to come back the same way, possibly in the dark. Today, the bridge is safe.

The observation platform, or gazebo, is a fine resting point. It has shade, benches and a million dollar view. The breeze coming off the prairie is refreshing and smells of swamp. The gazebo is a great place to get some thinking done while enjoying an adult beverage. The birding can be spectacular. Sandhill crane, blue heron, egrets, bald eagle, osprey and hawks are some of the marquee species that can be spotted. Also, there are loads of ducks and other waterfowl.

Hike the boardwalk. It's in surprisingly good shape, despite the bird poop and prairie flora gradually taking charge. Keep your eyes on the water. You may be treated to a glimpse of an otter, turtle or, of course, alligator.

At the end of the boardwalk is a small platform with a bench. You are at prairie central, and there are sights in every direction. If you stay for sunset, the cacophony of frogs, crickets and whatever else lives out there can be mind-boggling.

On my most recent trip to the Ocklawaha Prairie, I was relaxing at the gazebo and sipping a cup of wine when an odd-looking young fellow with spiked hair and thick glasses joined me. It was nearly sunset and getting chilly. I was slightly annoyed by the intrusion, but gracious.

"Care for a cup of wine?" I offered.

"Sure," he said. "Thanks."

He was lugging an impressive-looking leather briefcase slung over his shoulder. After a few sips of wine, he took out a writing pad and started to jot down notes. I gazed at the prairie and ignored him. He kept glancing up in my direction, and I sensed there was something he wanted to share.

I finally broke down and asked, "What are you writing?"

He seized the opportunity and handed me a business card. It read, "James E. Lindsay – Bigfoot Researcher," and had an imprint of the famous 1966 Roger Patterson photo of the big hairy guy. He proceeded to explain that he was investigating a recent Bigfoot sighting.

"Here?" I said. "On the prairie?"

"Yep."

He related the tale of an elderly couple from Belleview (a town about 10 miles away) who had spotted two Bigfoot a month earlier from the boardwalk. Their story was considered credible, not only because they were respected retired schoolteachers who went straight to the local police with their claim, but also because they told nearly identical versions while separated by the police. Plus, they had no monetary or other ulterior motives, and wanted to remain anonymous.

James was examining the prairie at the exact time the sighting had taken place, and was later going to meet with the couple in Belleview for an interview.

I grinned at him. "What do you think really happened?"

He put on a stone face and informed me there have been at least twelve credible sightings of Bigfoot in the Ocala National Forest, including a 1978 sighting by a Salt Springs Baptist minister. In fact, Seminole Indians spoke of a furry marauder prior to the 1835

Second Seminole Indian War, and current forest dwellers often refer to the legend of a "skunk ape."

He said, "The Ocklawaha Prairie would make an ideal habitat for Bigfoot because of the many near-inaccessible sections."

I yawned. "I guess."

"Google our website. You'll become a believer."

"Doubt it," I said.

He packed up his gear and left in a huff. The sun had set and the swamp noises intensified. I was alone in an area where two adult Bigfoot had recently been spotted frolicking near the boardwalk.

Bigfoot, I thought. Yeah, right.

I corked my wine and yelled, "Hey, James, wait up."

Hike # 2

Salt Springs River Trail

"No one should be able to enter a wilderness by mechanical means."
—Garrett Hardin

Directions – Go 0.5 miles south of Salt Springs on U.S. 19. Look for signs. Parking lot is on the left (east) side of highway.

Salt Springs River Trail is a 2.2-mile roundtrip loop that takes you to the Salt Springs River observation deck. It's an easy hike. Even though it's a short nature trail, easily accessed off a major highway, you will probably be the only hiker in the vicinity. Bring bug spray, even in the winter.
The trail winds through sand pine and scrub habitat. Several comfortable benches are placed strategically at intervals. There are hardwood hammocks, loblolly and slash pine, flatwoods, bayhead, myrtle oak, palm and cypress. The smells from the

swamp, river and pine needles can be overwhelming. Sniff the air for an approaching rain.

On the trail, watch for gopher tortoise and white tail deer. The trail is located just north of a major bear sanctuary. Keep your eyes open and stay alert.

Near the end of the loop, a spur trail leads to a boardwalk that spans a wetlands and ends at the observation deck. A large grove of Sabal palm (Florida's state tree) is an extra treat. The view of Salt Springs River, or run, is spectacular.

At the observation deck, watch for blue heron, limpkin and diving osprey. Bald eagles patrol the skies. Dragonflies like to perch on the reeds or land on your toes, a sure sign of a pristine water system. Fifty-two million gallons of water a day flow out of Salt Springs and feed the river. Watch for alligators sunning themselves on the flattened grass at the water's edge. Wave to the occasional boater.

William Bartram visited Salt Springs in 1774 and described it as an "amazing crystal fountain which meanders six miles through emerald meadows, pouring its limpid waters into the great Lake George." Later, English poet Samuel Taylor Coleridge set his epic poem *Kubla Khan* in a surreal landscape inspired by Bartram's description of Salt Springs published in *Travels* in 1791. Coleridge described Alph, the sacred river, as gushing forth from a "mighty crystal fountain amid dancing rocks." Coleridge continued to echo Bartram by having his fantasy river "five miles meandering with a mazy motion, through wood and dale the sacred river ran."

    This hike may not inspire you to write great poetry, but like Bartram you are sure to enjoy the crystal waters, the river's mazy motion and the inspiring beauty of Salt Springs.

Hike # 3

Land Bridge Trail

"Nothing like a nighttime stroll to give you ideas."
—Madeye Moody

Directions – Drive west out of Ocala on Highway 200 for 2 miles. Turn left on CR 475. After traveling 7 miles south, look for trailhead signs on the right (west).

As you drive south on CR 475 toward the Land Bridge trailhead, you are in for a special treat. CR 475 is a Marion County designated scenic highway. Huge oaks with draping Spanish moss line the two-lane road which runs past beautiful horse farms. Ocala is the thoroughbred horse capital of the south.

Marion County's scenic highway program is a superb idea. The program chooses the prettiest roads in the county and does not allow any development or changes except resurfacing. Unfortunately, unscrupulous developers, pretending to be defenders of property rights and growth management, make annual assaults on the program so they can line their pockets with the profits from unneeded malls, gated subdivisions and general urban sprawl. Marion County citizens must be on a constant vigil to protect and enforce their far-sighted scenic highway program from such greedy scoundrels.

The Land Bridge trail is a 2-mile roundtrip hike to a unique bridge over Interstate 75. It is the only land bridge that crosses an interstate in the nation. Other trail bridges, such as the ones for the Appalachian Trail, cross interstates but they are paved crossings. The land bridge in south Marion County is surfaced with dirt and has live shrubs and trees growing on its border.

The trail passes through a forest of ancient live oak. It traverses a portion of North Florida that appears much the same as it did when the Seminole war chief Osceola roamed the area in the 1830s. There are dozens of places to stop, not for a rest, but to gaze and admire. The area is achingly beautiful.

My favorite landmark on the trail is a monster live oak that boasts a natural throne chair. Have a seat and be a king or queen for a day.

At the land bridge, you can look down on six lanes of cars zooming north and south on Interstate 75, while standing among shrubs and trees with your hiking boots in the dirt. On my first visit to the land bridge, I considered waving to the passing motorists until I imagined bold headlines in the morning newspaper;

"Nitwit On Land Bridge Causes Massive Pile-Up And Twelve Hour Delay On I-75." I vetoed the idea. Then, to my amazement, drivers started to wave at me. At first, when I refused to wave back, they started blinking their headlights and honking their horns. I began to wave enthusiastically; it would have been rude not to acknowledge their greetings.

To the west of the land bridge there are two options, a pleasant bike path to SW 49th Avenue or a section of the Florida Trail marked by red blazes. If you decide to continue your hike, take the Florida Trail.

On the bike path, testosterone-crazed mountain biker's sail down the hill from the bridge at top speed while yelling their fool heads off for you to get out of the way. Please, you must fight the urge to throw an elbow and knock them on their asses.

On the Florida Trail, even though there aren't many compelling sights on this section, you will at least discover solitude.

The Land Bridge is located on a conservation preserve known as The Greenway. The Greenway is made up of Federal decommissioned land from the now-defunct Cross Florida Barge Canal. As loony as this idea sounds, in the 1930s the U.S. Army Corps of Engineers was authorized to construct a barge canal across the state of Florida, using several rivers including the St. Johns and Ocklawaha. The idiocy of the plan is beyond comprehension. Not only would the project ruin the rivers involved, it would also contaminate the Florida aquifer, which is an underground layer of porous limestone and rock that holds and filters the water that feeds our springs and lakes, and provides Floridians with their water supply.

On January 19, 1971, President Richard M. Nixon, in his finest environmental action, signed an executive order suspending further work on the canal. On January 22, 1991, Florida Governor Lawton Chiles signed a resolution that ultimately decommissioned the barge canal project and led to the creation of the Cross Florida Greenway State Recreation and Conservation Area.

Now for the real hero.

Micanopy resident, and perhaps Florida's greatest environmental activist, Marjorie Harris Carr, with help from her husband Archie, led a successful campaign to halt the barge canal and turn the property over to the state of Florida. Ms. Carr's previous efforts included helping to establish Paynes Prairie State Park and the restoration of Lake Alice on the campus of the University of Florida in Gainesville. Her greatest dream, however, was for the total restoration of the Ocklawaha River, which unfortunately still requires much work and effort from environmental organizations if the river is ever going to be restored to its natural course and previous glory.

In 1998, one year after Ms. Carr passed away at the age of 82, the greenway was officially renamed the Marjorie Harris Carr Cross Florida Greenway in her honor and memory.

Hike # 4

Lake Eaton and Sinkhole Trail

> "*The greatest way into the universe is through a forest wilderness.*"
> —John Muir

Directions – From Ocala, drive east on SR 40 for 5 miles and turn left on CR 314. Travel 8 miles and begin to look for signs for FR 50 and Lake Eaton Sinkhole. Follow signs to the trailhead on the left (east) side of the road.

Two trails at one trailhead. What a treat! Each trail is about 2 miles roundtrip, so if you hike them on the same day, your total mileage will be 4.3 miles.

Lake Eaton Sinkhole trail is to the east. It's 0.8 miles to the sink. The hole is about 80 feet deep and 450 feet across. It's not as big as Devil's Millhopper in Gainesville, but impressive nonetheless. Also, at the

Lake Eaton sink there is no swarm of tourists like the ones that gather at the Millhopper.

The hike is mostly through a scrub forest with sand pine. The Ocala National Forest has the largest stand of sand pine in the world. Several varieties of oak also inhabit the woods. Rusty Lyonia, which arcs its crooked branches over the trail, is known as "crooked wood." Strolling under the crooked wood adds to a sense of Hansel and Gretel wonderment to the trail, especially at night.

The kiosk at the top of the sinkhole also serves as a shelter, which is good to know if an afternoon squall rolls in. Linger at the top and read about the sinkhole at the kiosk. Lean over the wooden fence and gaze down into the sink in order to get a feel for this geological wonder. A wooden staircase leads to the bottom where there is an observation deck. No matter what season, it is always at least five degrees cooler on the deck.

Litterbugs compel me to wish that authorities hadn't banned the practice of public whippings on the town square. On a recent trip to the sinkhole, I sat on the deck with a glass of wine in hand, and suddenly discovered a dozen or more beer cans scattered about the sink. It was obvious that a group of pointy-headed cretins had sat at the same spot and hurled their empties in all directions. I climbed over the railing and picked up a total of sixteen cans. Back on the deck, I crushed them with my boot and stuffed them into my pack.

Take the long way back to the parking lot, not the 0.5-mile shortcut. It's a 1.2- mile hike and well worth it. Listen and watch for scrub jays. Silk Bay trees are abundant on this section of trail, and the slightly floral scent is considered aroma-therapeutic. Breathe deeply. Stiff breezes coming in off the Gulf of Mexico fifty miles to the west stir up the scent and create a refreshing experience.

Back at the parking lot, cross the road and hike downhill on the 2.3-mile Lake Eaton loop trail. Yes, I said downhill, which means there is a slight uphill on the return trip. Try to control your laughter. Anyone not from Florida will probably not even notice the ascent.

As you hike the trail, you will encounter three newly renovated boardwalks that lead to observation decks on the lake. Each deck provides a view of the lake with its own unique perspective and personality. As you hike, watch out for large Golden Orb spiders. Though scary looking, they are harmless, but you can still get a face-full of sticky web if you're not paying attention.

Pamphlets recommend hiking the loop counter-clockwise. Balderdash! I prefer clockwise because the observation decks become progressively better going in that direction.

After 0.5 miles, the first boardwalk and deck are on the left in a shaded cove with excellent opportunities to see alligators. The lake view is limited, however, and the mosquitoes will be at their most ferocious.

The next boardwalk and deck is the largest of the three and has expansive views of the lake. Although the views are stunning, there is no shade and the public boat ramp and fishing dock are visible on the other side of the lake.

Head north. As you hike deep inside the woods toward the final boardwalk and deck, you will pass stately loblolly pine and cabbage palm. This area is the most scenic part of the loop, and you will be able to catch glimpses of the sun glistening on the lake through the trees. Watch for bear. If they're around, this is the place they'll be.

The final boardwalk and deck are my favorites. The deck is smaller than the middle one, but it's in a much more remote section of the lake and has better views. Sunsets over this fresh but dark water lake can be awe-inspiring. I do admit, however, that if I fell off the deck, I'd attempt to walk on water. There are a ton of gators and snakes skimming the surface. In fact, wave a flashlight to spot the red gator eyes among the lily pads.

Following sunset, hike out the final 0.8 miles using the flashlight.

Hike # 5

Chornobyl Memorial Forest

*"The greatest wonder is that we can
see these trees and not wonder."*
—Ralph Waldo Emerson

Directions – From Ocala, drive east on SR 40 for 12 miles to Four Corners. Turn right (south) on SR 314A. In 7 miles, turn right (south) over the Ocklawaha River Bridge. Trailhead parking is 2 miles on the right (west) side of the road.

The hike around the Chornobyl Memorial Forest is a pleasant 3.8-mile loop on a 314-acre site that was once a melon field. It is 0.5 miles to the start of the loop. The forest is dedicated to the memory of the victims from the Chornobyl nuclear power plant accident in 1986. Chornobyl is the Ukrainian spelling. Since the disaster occurred in the

Ukraine, it was decided the Ukrainian spelling would be more respectful than the more familiar Chernobyl.

I don't like nuclear power plants; they are simply too dangerous. One bad accident negates all the good points. First there was the accident at Three Mile Island in Pennsylvania, and more recently the Fukushima disaster in Japan. Chornobyl was sandwiched in between. Would you want to raise your children a few blocks away from a nuclear power plant?

Nuclear waste remains radioactive for thousand of years and not one nuclear genius has figured out what to do with it. No state or nation wants to store the waste. Presently, the Federal government pays Nevada (which has a population of 37 outside Las Vegas and Reno) to keep it.

In April 1986, the world's worst nuclear power plant accident to date occurred at the Chornobyl power plant near Pry Priat, Ukraine, and in the vicinity of Kiev, a city of four million people. Thousands perished, and tens of thousands developed health problems. Presently, the area surrounding the damaged plant is a ghostly wasteland. It is said reindeer, as far away as Lapland, have been born with three legs. The legacy of horror will infect generations.

Many Ukrainians, who had formerly lived in vast forested regions, were forced to move into urban areas following the disaster. Survivors originated the idea of a forested preserve to be set aside as a memorial for all that was lost. The Chornobyl Committee sought worldwide for this memorial forest.

On March 29, 1996, United States and Ukrainian officials, with the cooperation of the Chornobyl Committee of Washington, D.C., and using funds donated by the American Forests Organization, chose the state of Florida as the site and decided to create a memorial forest in Ocklawaha, of all places, to remember the victims, survivors, and environmental ruination of the Ukrainian terrain.

The St. Johns River Water Management District, or SJRWMD, planted over 150,000 longleaf pines, a species itself decimated by unregulated logging, to symbolize the importance of renewal, rebirth and restoration. Many of the trees are twenty to thirty feet tall today. Harry Dean, executive director of SJRWMD, said, "This forest serves as a timeless reminder that humanity has the power to either nurture or destroy the environment."

Hiking the 3.8-mile trail can also help with the renewal of your soul. Besides the lovely forest, there are gray fox, bobcat, gopher tortoise and bear roaming the area. I found numerous bear tracks less than one hundred yards into the hike.

Tip # 1: Stay on the edge of the trail. Much of the center is sandy.

Tip # 2: Go right on the loop. After 0.7 miles, the trail makes a sweeping left turn. You'll see three gnarled and crooked live oak trees near the remnants of an old corral. Here is an ideal place to spread out the blanket and pour a beer, glass of Cabernet or vodka tonic. The loop continues around the thick and dark memorial forest. As a special treat, bushwhack into the woods, if you dare.

Tip # 3: After your hike, head north on CR 314A to Duck's Dam Diner for the best hamburgers in the state. There's a story of a middle school student who was asked by an assistant principal what he did over the weekend. He proudly replied, "I ate at the Dam Diner," and promptly received three swats.

Hike # 6

Sunnyhill Restoration Area

"I never liked formal gardens. I liked wild nature. It's just the wilderness instinct in me, I guess."

—Walt Disney

Directions – From Ocala drive east on SR 40 for 12 miles. Turn right (south) on CR 314A at Four Corners. Drive south for 9 miles and turn right on SE 182nd Avenue Road. Look for parking lot signs 2 miles on the right (west).

Sunnyhill Restoration Area is 4,505 acres of reclaimed muck farms on the banks of the Ocklawaha River. This section of the river is a straight, dredged-out canal. The original bed of the Ocklawaha is on the property, and restoring the river to its natural course is the primary goal of the restoration area.

From the late 1800s to the 1930s, before construction on the Cross Florida Barge Canal was begun, specially built paddleboats, extra tall and slender, plied the waters of the Ocklawaha. Starting from Jacksonville, the paddleboats cruised up the St. Johns River, and entered the lower Ocklawaha in order to bring tourists to the headwaters of the fabulous Silver Springs. The boats traveled south while heading upriver since both the St. Johns and Ocklawaha run north, like the famous Nile River in North Africa.

>(North Florida joke:
>Why does the St. Johns River flow north?
>Because Georgia sucks!)

During this era, the Ocklawaha was considered one of the top ten most beautiful rivers in America. While the northern section of the river, from SR 40 to the St. Johns, is still beautiful, its waters are murky and no longer crystal clear. The southern section is a dredged-out canal with a lock. On the Sunnyhill property it is possible to hike or bike almost 10 miles along the canal section of the river. Comparing these miles of straight canal to the gorgeous, snake-like course of the real river makes a convincing argument for removing the lock at Moss Bluff and restoring the river to its natural course.

The hike at Sunnyhill is an easy 2-mile roundtrip to a primitive backpacking site. From the parking lot, hike straight out for 0.8 miles, and at the first fork turn left. The campsite is 0.2 miles from the fork. At the campsite, other trails fan out in several directions if you choose to hike further.

The Sunnyhill primitive campsite is situated in the middle of an ancient oak hammock It has sheltered tables, benches and a fire pit. It is a startlingly beautiful oasis, and a great spot to relax and enjoy adult activities.

You want to see bear? I can practically guarantee you will catch a glimpse of a bear. I have spotted bear every time I've visited Sunnyhill, and not just one. Also, these are good bear. They keep their distance and run if you get too close.

Be careful. The watery areas are snake-infested, especially with cottonmouth, or moccasin. Watch your step. Cottonmouths have an attitude and lack a sense of humor. Also, no matter how inviting it may appear, never drink any Florida surface water without boiling or purifying it. Even then, I wouldn't drink it. One case of dysentery is more than enough. Always pack more water than you think you will need.

At the campsite, there is an old-fashioned water pump for rinsing dishes or washing hands. There is a sign that reads, "Do Not Drink - Water Is Not Potable." On one of my hikes to Sunnyhill, I brought along two friends. One of them pumped some water into a cup and tasted it. We'll call him John.

"I think we can drink it," John proclaimed. "This water is pure."

My other friend was a retired major in the U.S. Air Force. We'll call him Rob.

"What do you think, Rob?" John asked.

Major Rob frowned and said, "Read the sign, dumbass."

That remains my advice. And since we're on the subject, let me pass along this wisdom from the great Harry Crews:

> I bent down once to drink from a stream high in the mountains on the trail, and just as I was about to, as they say, *slake* my thirst, I saw a little sign put up by the Forestry Service or somebody that said: "DO NOT DRINK. CONTAMINATED WITH UNTREATED WASTE." I always love that: *untreated* waste. As though I might enjoy—perhaps really like—to drink *treated* waste. But, alas why dwell upon it? The planet is tired and dying. I understand, though, that even the most pessimistic predictions give us (or at least a few of us) another million years or so.

After relaxing at the campsite, venture east and try your luck at locating Ghost Pond. I call it Ghost Pond because sometimes it's there and sometimes it's not. You may be required to do a little bushwhacking, but it's well worth it if the pond happens to be there. It's a superb spot to watch the sunset. If the pond is gone, and there is only a dried grass indentation, that means the ghost is on the move.

Hike # 7

Marshall Swamp

I can only meditate when I'm walking. When I stop, I cease to think. My mind only works with my legs."

—Jean Jacques Rousseau

Directions – From Ocala, drive east on SR 40 for 5 miles. Turn right (south) on CR 35 (Baseline Road) in Silver Springs. Drive 1.5 miles to CR 314 (Sharps Ferry Road). Turn left (east) and continue 2 miles to trailhead parking on the right (south).

If you hike the Marshall Swamp trail late in the afternoon, I can almost guarantee you'll have the trail to yourself. This is a primordial swamp trail. The sun rarely touches the ground. It is 2.5 miles one-way, so hike as far as you want, knowing you'll have to return the same way. The trail is well marked and finely crafted, using a gravel cover so hikers' feet won't get wet or muddy, even during the rainy season.

The Marshall Swamp is a smorgasbord of trees, with chestnut, live oak, maple, cypress, sweetgum, cabbage palm and ancient loblolly pine. It can be a dark and forbidding place, with a Grimm Brothers type of spookiness. I recommend against bushwhacking.

Historically, the Ocklawaha River Raid, a Civil War skirmish, took place in March 1865. A small Union force raided several plantations in the Marshall Swamp, using gunboats off the Ocklawaha River. When the raiding party fell upon the Marshall Plantation, owned by the widow of Jehu Foster Marshall, a Confederate colonel killed in the Second Battle of Manassas, the Ocala home guard militia counterattacked and chased off the raiders. The plantation, however, was burned to the ground. This was the only Civil War action to occur in Marion County. A local legend claims that ghosts of the fallen Confederate soldiers still roam the swamp in the evening mists. The Marshall Swamp is certainly an ideal home for wandering spirits.

Also, historically, the swamp was a haven for wolves, although wolves are now extinct in the state of Florida. Howls coming out of the swamp today are from coyotes. Conservation officials have recently considered reintroducing the eastern red wolf to the Marshall Swamp.

Another cry that once echoed through the swamp was Tarzan's signature yodel-yell. Although most of the Tarzan movie footage was filmed along the Silver River two miles away, many of the scenes with

Johnny Weissmuller swinging from tree to tree were taken in the Marshall Swamp. The filmmakers used actual local grapevines, which were as thick as boa constrictors.

A half-mile into the trail, there is a short boardwalk that leads to an observation deck. The deck overlooks a small pond and wetland. It's a perfect setting for reading or just listening to the sounds of the swamp. Though the wetland view is rather unspectacular, sunsets on the deck can be inspiring. Also, there is a short loop trail around the pond.

In the 1990s, the Ocala City Council suggested a plan to pump the city's treated sewage into the Marshall Swamp, claiming the purifying nature of the swamp would filter the nitrates and harmful bacteria before they reached the Ocklawaha River. The idea was colossally ignorant, considering both the Silver and Ocklawaha rivers are being choked to death by exotic weeds caused by nitrates and sewage seeping into their waters. Fortunately, local environmental groups brought the project to a grinding halt.

Hike # 8

St. George Island State Park
Gap Point Trail

"The urge within me to be in the woods and fields or along a stream is such a strong and pleasant desire that I have no inclination to withstand it."
—Jimmy Carter

Directions – From Apalachicola drive east on U.S. 98 for 2 miles over the bay bridge. In Eastpoint, turn right (south) and head over the causeway to St. George Island. On the island, turn left (east) and follow signs to the state park. Go to the campground and park at the end of the loop.

St. George Island State Park is a stunningly pristine park, prettier than many Caribbean islands. It's location on the so-called "Forgotten Coast" helps keep the crowds to a minimum. With the exception of St. Joseph Peninsula, this park has the finest campground in the southeast.

There are over ten miles of isolated and nearly empty white-sand beaches on this 1,962-acre barrier island. Gap Point trailhead is at the back of the park's campground. The tiny parking area has room for only four cars, but I've never seen it full. If the lot is full, park at the entrance to the campground and walk to the trailhead.

Gap Point Trail is a windy 2.5-mile stroll through a beautiful forest of pine flats and coastal scrub with a signpost and bench every half-mile. The trail pleads with a hiker to linger and enjoy. Winds come off the bay to rustle the needles of the slash pine and cool your face. Scrub jay rules the roost. At 0.5 miles into the hike, you can hook up with the East Slough Trail and hike over a forested dune. There is a wooden bridge over the East Slough that offers a spectacular view. I recommend the spot for an adult beverage.

I'd heard rumors about bear in the wilderness tract at Gap Point. The bear supposedly swim across the bay, eat all the campground scraps and swim back to the mainland. Nonsense, I scoffed. Then a ranger confirmed the story.

At the end of the trail is a grassy point set aside for primitive camping. There are tables and fire pits, but no water. On the southern side of the point, you can wander along the shore of East Slough. To the west and north is wilderness along Apalachicola Bay, which contains one of the most famous oyster beds in the world. Explore the bay side leisurely. It is a tropical paradise and the hours seem to melt away.

In November 2012, I solo backpacked Gap Point Trail. I called ahead for reservations at 1-800-326-3527 and was told there would be seven other backpackers on the site. It was a crisp sunny day. I set up my tent on the grassy point at water's edge and explored the East Slough.

No other campers showed up.

At about 4:00 p.m. the winds off the bay began to pick up unexpectedly and appeared to gain strength by the minute. When it was time for sunset, the temperature had plummeted into the low 40s, and I was suddenly experiencing a nightmare gale force storm. The bay had four-foot whitecaps and my face was frozen. It was a tad warmer inside the tent, but the ferocious wind bent the poles and caused the sides to slap me in my face. I feared the tent would sail away if I weren't sitting in it.

It was 5:00 p.m. I certainly did not want to stay in my tiny backpacking tent until morning, but the wind and cold temperatures made life on the point miserable. It would be dark in thirty minutes.

Decision time. Should I endure this agony or get the hell out? I wanted out. Decision number two. Should I break camp or batten down the hatches and leave my stuff? I could retrieve it the next morning. If I broke camp, it would mean an extra thirty minutes on the trail in the dark. It was now in the thirties. I decided to leave it.

On my way out, as I shined my flashlight into the woods, I noticed a small clearing among the tall slash pine. Though the wind was still fierce, it was not nearly as bad as on the point. It was now pitch black. Decision number three. Should I keep hiking or spend the night in the clearing? I went back to the gear, unpegged the tent with everything inside, and dragged it to the new campsite. I put on my North Face jacket and gloves, sat in front of the tent, and cracked the label on a bottle of Jim Beam. I was determined to enjoy the evening, dadgummit.

  Which I did. I even slept well. In fact, I was still in my sleeping bag when the ranger arrived in the morning. He had hiked out to make certain I survived the frigid night. He told me the temperature had dipped to 27 degrees. I told him I was okay, thanked him for checking on me, and began getting my gear together.

  After hiking out, I drove into Apalachicola. This historic town was featured in the 1997 film *Ulee's Gold*, starring Peter Fonda in an academy award nominated performance. I explored the town, enjoyed a splendid dinner at Boss Oyster on the Apalachicola River, and treated myself to a night at the beautifully restored Coombs House Inn, a primo bed and breakfast.

  I know, the trials and tribulations of backpacking.

Hike # 9

Tate's Hell
High Bluff Coastal Trail

"Work sucks! I'm going hiking."
—L. Larson

Directions – High Bluff Coastal Trail is off U.S. 98, 2.7 miles west of Carrabelle. Look for signs to parking lot on the north side of highway.

Around 1875, 45 year-old Cebe Tate set off into a wetland area in search of a panther, which had been killing off his cattle. He was armed with a rifle and accompanied by two hunting dogs. After searching for the panther for a few hours, Tate got separated from his dogs and became hopelessly lost and disoriented. In an attempt to not panic, he took a rest at the base of a large cypress knee and was promptly bitten by a rattlesnake. Eaten up by mosquitoes and with the snake venom causing severe delirium, Tate wandered in the swamp for three days. When he finally emerged somewhere north of Carrabelle, over 25 miles from his home, he approached two men and said, "My name is Tate, and I've just been in hell." After speaking those words, he fell dead at the men's feet.

The tale of Tate reminds me vaguely of what Ebenezer Bryce said after he was lost for days in the canyon that bears his name—"Tough place to find a stray."

Who are these men? How did they become so resolute and taciturn? If I were lost in Tate's Hell or Bryce Canyon, I'd be howling for my mommy.

The High Bluff Coastal Trail is a 1.2-mile hike to a lovely wooded site with a picnic table and open view of the swamp. Tall pines poke holes in the sky. Breezes coming in off the gulf cause the pine trees to sway and glisten. There are few things sweeter than the smell and sound of pine needles in a wind. Look for deer, bobcat and bald eagle. Listen for pileated woodpeckers, and smell the mint and rosemary. This is true wilderness.

Back on U.S. 98, between Eastpoint and Carrabelle, take SR 65 north and follow the signs into the Tate's Hell High Bluff tract. Turn right on Drawbridge Road and follow signs to the Ralph G. Kendrick Dwarf Cypress Boardwalk parking lot.

Be careful if the area is wet.

The Dwarf Cypress Boardwalk is an easy but highly rewarding 0.25-mile hike to a rare and impressive stand of 15-foot-high, centuries old, dwarf cypress.

On the drive back to U.S. 98, I discovered a small marsh pond with a rickety dock about ten feet above the water. The pond appeared to be an old lime pit. At least half of the slats on the rickety dock were missing. I parked the truck and walked to the edge of the pit. Black shimmering water filled the pond. The steep banks prevented me from going down to the shore.

I looked at the dock again, and could almost hear the infamous last words, "Here, hold my beer." I crawled out on all fours. Once I got out over the water, a fall wouldn't be the end of the world, I'd just get wet. In a moment or two, I was sitting on the last board, legs dangling, enjoying the view.

Then I looked down. I was able to make out the vague outline of an alligator, mostly submerged, but still visible in the dark water. His head was the only part of his body out of the water.

"Oh, crap," I said.

Did I say alligator? This 14-foot monster was a modern day Godzilla. Then, I noticed he was glaring at me. If I fell I would land smack dab on his tail. Suddenly, a wind blew and rattled the dock. The board I was sitting on wobbled. I broke into a sweat and started to panic. Slowly, I crawled back to shore with a death grip on each slat.

I didn't breathe easily until I was safely locked in my truck with the windows rolled up.

Hike # 10

St. Joseph Peninsula State Park Peninsula Trail

"In the wilderness I sense the miracle of life, and behind it our scientific accomplishments fade to trivia."
—Charles Lindbergh

Directions – From Apalachicola, drive west on U.S. 98 for 14 miles. Turn left onto CR 30, and after 14 more miles take a left at CR 30E. Follow signs to the State Park and trailhead parking.

I have trails from four State Parks in this book yet, ironically, I don't like to recommend the State Parks for hiking. North Florida State Parks are as nice and pretty as any state parks in the nation, but because of the stringent rules and regulations, crowds, and officious rangers, the parks tend to be somewhat restrictive for the free-spirited hiker. They don't even allow leashed dogs on the trails. In winter, most of the parks lock their front gates at 5:00 p.m. If you miss closing time and drive up to a locked gate, you will be met by a grumpy ranger. But St. George Island, St. Joseph Peninsula, Paynes Prairie, and Silver Springs are such spectacular North Florida parks that I would be guilty of gross negligence if I excluded them.

  At St. Joseph Peninsula there are incredible coastal hikes, both on the gulf and bay side. As you head toward the park on CR 30E, Cape San Blas juts west while the road up the peninsula turns north. Thus, the peninsula runs north and south, an oddity along the panhandle coast, and CR 30E ends at the state park's entrance. This makes the western gulf beaches in the park outstanding for sunsets, while the eastern bay side is great for sunrises. At the end of CR 30E is a 1,900-acre wilderness preserve that occupies the entire northern tip of the peninsula. It is a 6-mile hike to the point and 6 more miles back, or you could hike out only as far as you desire.

  One of the nicest rangers in the southeast works at St. Joseph Peninsula State Park. I made the colossally stupid mistake of pulling off the road and parking my truck off the pavement. Immediately, my tires sank a foot into the sand. I'd still be digging out today if that ranger had not come to my rescue and towed the truck back onto the highway. He would accept no money, and I wasn't even inside the State Park boundary. Needless to say, do not drive vehicles onto the sand.

There are three ways to hike on the peninsula—bay, gulf or interior. You can hike up the interior and return on either the bay or gulf sides. The interior has pine woods, shade and fantastic scenery, but the thick sand makes hiking on the trail a severe workout. I suggest taking the bay trail on the way out, then cross over the interior to the gulf side for your return. That way you can briefly experience the interior's dunes and woods. The sand on both coasts is hard packed near the water. On your return trip along the gulf, the sound of the waves is soothing, and you may catch a sunset. Sunsets on the gulf beach or on top of a dune can be surreal and life altering. St. Joseph Peninsula State Park is the only place where I have witnessed the legendary "green flash." If you don't know about this rare phenomenon, I recommend John D. MacDonald's novel *A Flash of Green*.

The coastline along the bay is extraordinarily picturesque. I'd say it has a Caribbean flavor, only different. It's North Florida. The view across the bay toward the town of Port St. Joe is gorgeous. It wasn't always so. Years ago, there was the hulking, smoky and stinky St. Joe paper mill. But the St. Joe Paper Company tore the mill down and helped the town replace it with a public marina. Today the bay view is pristine and the town of Port St. Joe has reinvented itself and is a delight to visit. For decades the St. Joe Paper Company has been a responsible manager and steward of tens of thousands of acres on the Florida panhandle, and makes certain that areas where trees have been harvested are immediately re-forested and renewed.

After you've hiked your fill on the bay side, cross the interior to hook up with the gulf. The return hike along the gulf has an immaculate, sugar-white sand shoreline that was rated the number one beach in the nation in 2002 by the famous Dr. Beach, Stephen Parker Leatherman, who assigns his personal ratings each year. Dr. Leatherman is an author, coastal ecologist and professor at Florida International University in Miami.

The sand dunes inside the interior preserve are the highest in the United States. Bobcat, deer, fox and coyote are common. I once thought I saw a mongoose, but a ranger insisted it was a bald squirrel, which is common on the cape. The park is also a much-needed resting spot for dozens of migrating birds and butterflies.

After your hike, I recommend you stay in the park. There are pleasant cabins for rent and the number two campground is one of the finest in Florida.

Hike # 11

Paynes Prairie State Park Bolen Bluff Trail

"Sometimes when you lose your way, you find yourself."
—Mary Hale

Directions – 8 miles south of Gainesville on U.S. 441, or 27 miles north of Ocala. Parking lot is on the east side of the highway.

Bolen Bluff is one of three trails within Paynes Prairie State Park that are included in this book. The other two hikes are Cone Dike and Chacala Pond. To get to the Bolen Bluff trailhead, you need not enter the State Park because Bolen Bluff is a spur trail off U.S. 441.

Bolen is probably the name of an early family of pioneers who lived on the south rim of the prairie.

In my opinion the Bolen Bluff Trail is the most beautiful trail in North Florida. Every time an out-of-state friend comes to visit, I take them to Bolen Bluff. Immediately upon leaving the small dirt parking lot, a hiker is immersed in countless groves of live oak with Spanish moss draped from their branches. In the early morning or late afternoon, the area can be hauntingly beautiful. Also, along the trail, there are sweetgum, hickory, magnolia and several species of palm. The 1.2-mile hike to the bluff is an excellent example of "The Real Florida." It is also a perfect sampling of how North Florida appeared to the indigenous people before the arrival of Europeans.

About 200 yards into the hike, the trail splits into a loop. Choose either direction; just be certain to come back the other way. You don't want to miss any of the sights this trail has to offer. I could stroll along the Bolen Bluff loop every day for the rest of my life and be happy. There are many spots to relax and enjoy the surroundings. At the bluff, there is an incredible view of Paynes Prairie. Many hikers have compared the prairie to a wet African savannah. In fact, William Bartram called Paynes Prairie the Great Alachua Savannah.

Paynes Prairie was named after King Payne, a chief of the Seminoles, who was killed in a battle with American settlers near the Georgia border in 1812. Similar skirmishes caused Andrew Jackson to invade

Spanish Florida in 1818 with a force of 4,000 and initiate the First Seminole Indian War. At the conclusion of the war, Spain ceded Florida to the United States. At the time, the prairie was a large lake. It was also a lake nearly 300 years earlier when Spanish explorer Hernando De Soto camped along its shores in 1540, and when William Bartram visited in 1774.

On December 18, 1835, the first battle of the Second Seminole Indian War, known as the Battle of Black Point, occurred on Bolen Bluff. Florida militias, rather than Federal troops, were involved. A small force with wagon supplies was ambushed in the early morning. Six to eight Americans were killed and the wagons stolen. Two days later, a much larger Florida militias force recaptured the wagons at Black Point. On December 28, 1835, Indian agent Wiley Thompson, a former general and U.S. Congressman, was shot and killed by Osceola outside the ramparts of Fort King near Ocala, with a special rifle that had been given to Osceola as a gift by Thompson himself. On that same day, about forty miles south of Fort King, 107 reinforcements from Fort Brooke near Tampa, under the command of Major Francis Dade, were attacked and killed by Seminole warriors under the leadership of Micanopy, Alligator and Jumper. These incidents were the cause of the Second Seminole Indian War.

At Bolen Bluff, there is an open grassy knoll with a bench. This is a great spot to relax and view the prairie. A spur trail drops down into the prairie and leads to a small observation deck. Many times after work I have hiked to the deck to enjoy a sunset, and then hiked back to the bluff with a flashlight. The hike back in partial darkness is like being immersed in a primordial swamp with every type of reptile and insect noise imaginable. It's a great way to experience the atavistic fears of our early human ancestors who were not at the top of the food chain.

Careful: Wild Spanish horses still roam the prairie. Do not approach.

Special warning: Weekends are often crowded with students from the University of Florida. Early mornings or late afternoons on weekdays are the best times to visit the bluff.

Hike # 12

Paynes Prairie State Park Cone Dike Trail

"*A vigorous five-mile hike will do more good for all the unhappy but otherwise healthy adults than all the medicine and psychology in the world*"
—Paul Dudley White

Directions – 12 miles south of Gainesville, or 22 miles north of Ocala on U.S. 441. Look for signs to the entrance gate on the left (east) side of the highway. Drive 4 miles north to the parking lot.

If you want to see bison, alligator, bald eagle, wading birds and Spanish horses, the Cone Dike Trail inside Paynes Prairies State Park is your place. The trail does a right turn, a quick left and then another right in a straight shot for 4 miles, all within what William Bartram called the Great Alachua Savannah.

Some hikers find this trail long and boring. What planet do they come from? The only boring things in life are boring people. Since it is an 8-mile roundtrip hike, you can decide how far you wish to venture out, and then simply turn around.

Bring lots of water.

Also, either coming or going, be sure to stop at the fine visitor center and the three-story observation deck for long-range views of the prairie.

On a crisp winter's day, Cone Dike Trail may be the finest trail for viewing wildlife in North Florida. In winter the prairie grasses are lower so you can see for longer distances, and your chances of spotting wildlife improve dramatically. Bring binoculars for birding and long-range views of the bison.

Honest to God! Bison freely roam this prairie. There have been discussions about removing them, but so far that hasn't happened. At times, the bison and Spanish horses will block the trail, while at other times you'll be lucky to see them with binoculars. Do not approach them. If you can't walk around them, wait them out. They will move along eventually. Let me repeat, do not approach them or invade their space. Both species are bigger than you, and getting trampled would not be pleasant.

The wild horses on Paynes Prairie are descendants of the Florida cracker horses brought by the Spanish in the 1500s, and later abandoned in favor of larger animals in the next century. There are about 2,000 left in Florida with a sizable portion in Paynes Prairie.

 Besides a wide variety of birds, Cone Dike Trail is also famous for its seasonal butterflies. In order to experience the butterfly spectacle, however, you may have to brave warmer weather.

 Along the trail, alligator is still the king. I can almost guarantee you will see gators while hiking the Cone Dike Trail, often times sunning themselves on the actual trail. They generally will return to the prairie upon your approach. If they don't flee, the worst they might do is hiss loudly. Never do something stupid around an alligator. Regardless of its size, they all have teeth.

 After about 2.5 miles on the trail, you'll make a sharp right turn. Along this section you can actually find shade. For the next 1.5 miles you may feel like you're in Jurassic Park, with no civilization in sight. Pick any spot on the wide causeway trail for rest, relaxation and a picnic.

 After leaving the state park, visit the historic hamlet of Micanopy. If a little dirt were thrown over Main Street, you'd feel like you were transported back to the 19th century. In fact, filmmakers did just that for the 1983 movie *Cross Creek*, starring Rip Torn and Peter Coyote as locals, and Mary Steenburgen as author Marjorie Kinnan Rawlings. The historic storefronts appear much as they did in the 1800s. The 1991 movie

Doc Hollywood, starring Michael J. Fox and Woody Harrelson, was also filmed in town.

In 1539, Hernando De Soto noted a Timucuan Indian village on the site. Later, in 1774, William Bartram described a Seminole village named Cooscoowilla at the same locale.

In 1821, the newly constructed town of Micanopy became the first U.S. district settlement in the interior of the territory of Florida. The town was named after a fierce Seminole war chief, "to acknowledge his original authority of the land," wrote historian C.S. Monaco. Fort Defiance (1835-1836) and Fort Micanopy (1837-1843) were located nearby, and both played pivotal roles in the Second Seminole Indian War.

Today, Micanopy is at peace. Stroll down Main Street and take pictures. Visit the Herlong Mansion, now a fine Bed and Breakfast, and noted for hosting weddings. Shop for antiques or vintage books, and eat a sandwich, cookie or ice cream cone at one of the several cafes.

Hike # 13

Paynes Prairie State Park Chacala Pond Trail

"If you haven't seen anything incredible today, hike into a forest."
—Robo B.

Directions – Same as Cone Dike Trail, except after driving just one mile inside the state park, watch for signs for trailhead parking on the right.

The Chacala Pond Trail is a series of loops through a pristine pine forest with no views of Paynes Prairie. The trail definitely has its own unique personality. It is shady, quiet and soothing. Some sections have such thick woods that hikers will experience the "tunnel effect" while hiking.

There are loops A, B and C. The entire trail is 6.5 miles and can go up to 8 miles if you hike all the inner connections. Loop A is 2 miles, loop B, 1.5 miles, and loop C, 2.5 miles.

The terrain is a fine dry upland habitat with thick groves of slash pine. The bird population will make a racket. On loop C there is a short spur trail that leads to Chacala Pond. It is a spring-fed pond with no development. You can discover an excellent view of the pond if you climb up on the picnic table. Careful: the pond is a favorite gathering spot among snakes and gators. You may also run into some wriggling green "hanging caterpillars" that suspend themselves from the tree branches by using a thin filament. Watch for bald eagle, osprey and turkey vulture soaring over the pond.

In the woods, you may bump into whitetail deer, fox and gopher tortoise. Also, wild turkey abound. Wild turkeys are swift and dazzling creatures, either running or in flight. Their gobbling will excite the senses much like the cries of the loon. I'm one of the few supporters of Ben Franklin's nomination of the wild turkey as America's national symbol.

The solitude on the Chacala Pond Trail will renew the soul. However, on Saturdays in the fall, I discovered, Chacala Pond is a popular running trail for the University of Florida men's cross country team. (This is the university team that has boasted such excellent runners as Frank Shorter, Jack Bachelor and John L. Parker, who authored the cult classic *Once A Runner*.) Nine or ten runners may suddenly appear and gallop swiftly down the trail. You may see a future star or Olympian.

Loop B has a dandy primitive backpacking site. This is also a perfect place to wile away the hours reading, meditating or daydreaming. Build a small fire in the fire pit. Although I'm no longer a user, I recommend this spot for a moderate dose of marijuana. The mood of the nation over marijuana has finally turned the corner toward acceptance. The legal and political campaign against this mild, non-addicting drug not only boggles the mind, but has been foolhardy and illogical. Prohibition does not work. Didn't the U.S. Government learn any lessons with alcohol? The idiocy of Federal and state policies has been amazingly ineffective and impractical. Think of the amounts of manpower and money that have been wasted on law enforcement, court cases and incarceration.

Legalization means regulation, tax revenue and increased safety. It would also snatch control of distribution from the hands of oftentimes-violent criminals. Also, the many other uses of the product are rarely discussed. Besides the medical values, hemp can replace trees as a source for paper as well as contribute to the textile and clothing industries. In marijuana growing areas, the local economies would benefit. But, I digress.

Marijuana can make adult hiking a more pleasurable experience. Colorado has legalized it, and Colorado has some of the best hiking on the planet.

Before leaving the park, head over to Lake Wauburg. This is a beautiful spring-fed lake with a serious alligator population.

Hike # 14

Barr Hammock

*"The promised land always lies
on the other side of wilderness."*
—Havelock Ellis

Directions – Drive 10 miles south of Gainesville, or 26 miles north of Ocala, on U.S. 441. Turn west on Wacahoota Road and follow signs over I-75 to the parking lot.

Barr Hammock is a 5,700-acre site along the Paynes Prairie corridor, and was purchased and opened in 2013 by the Alachua County Forever Program for "the enjoyment of all." The Alachua County Forever Program is one of many Florida county programs, approved overwhelmingly by voters, to set a halfpenny tax aside in a trust for the purchase of unique and sensitive land for parks and preservation. The farsightedness of such programs, and the decisive action of voters, sets a positive example for all counties and states in America. Florida's population has exploded, and greedy developers who are not local residents, and have little concern for our sensitive environment, have invaded the state. Land purchase programs for wetlands, wildlife habitats and other unique settings for preservation should be initiated by all of Florida's 67 counties before it's too late. Most state and county governments are far too pro-development to carry the environmental torch.

Barr Hammock is nicknamed "the emerald necklace" because it connects several other prairies including Paynes and Tuscawilla. The trail is along an old levee road and loops 6.5 miles around a miraculously restored marsh. If you want to see alligator, snakes, otter, wading birds and raptors, this is your place.

Examples of some of the amusing signs at Barr Hammock (comments in italics are mine):

- Do Not Approach Alligators Blocking The Trail. *Duh!*
- For Your Own Safety, Do Not Enter The Marsh. *Double Duh!!*
- Do Not Molest The Snakes. *Huh? Sounds perverse.*
- Watch Out For Quicksand. *How about some signs pointing out the quicksand?*
- Visitors Who Remain After Hours Are Trespassing. *What?? It's our land.*

The trail is on a border dike, and except in extremely wet conditions is totally safe. Just don't be stupid. Gators do bask along the trail and snakes may be nearby. None will bother you if you don't bother them. The surface of the trail is generally grassy, but can get boggy after a hard rain.

The north levee has no shade, but offers impressive vistas over the marsh. I recommend hiking the north levee first. Hats, sunglasses and sunscreen, even during winter, are musts. There are nice benches along the trail on which to rest and observe the sights. The south levee is mostly shaded and gorgeous. There is a slow-moving stream on the south side of the trail that has otters. Also, you may see deer, fox, coyote, bobcat and the usual list of wading birds.

South and north trail extensions have signs that read CLOSED. Though I hesitate to encourage rule breaking, both trails have exceptional scenery and I found no discernible reasons for the closure.

Hike # 15

Pat's Island

*"Now my friends and passersby,
As you are now so once was I,
As I am now you soon will be,
Prepare for Heaven and follow me."*
—Sign at Long Cemetery

Directions – Drive east on SR 40 from Ocala for 28 miles. Turn left (north) on SR 19. Drive north for 7 miles. Look for signs near Silver Glen Springs. Turn left (west) on SR 46. Trail parking is 2 miles on the right (north).

The 3.5-mile loop trail that circles Pat's Island, and then follows Jody's Trace, is perhaps the wildest and most scenic section of the Ocala National Forest. It is named after Patrick Smith, who settled in the 1840s and became the area's first postmaster.

Pat's Island lies in the northern section of the 13,260-acre Juniper Prairie Wilderness designated in

1984. Juniper Prairie is one of 700 wilderness areas created by the Wilderness Act of 1964. The act designates areas for minimal human imprint, including no motorized vehicles (motorcycles, ATV's, etc.) or mechanized devices (bicycles), and no hunting. The areas should also remain roadless. When President Lyndon B. Johnson signed the act, he said, "If future generations are to remember us with gratitude rather than contempt, we must leave them a glimpse of the world as it was in the beginning, not just after we got through with it." Johnson was an environmental visionary. Currently, the Wilderness Act encompasses 109.5 million acres in 44 states and Puerto Rico, or 5% of the land in the United States.

In North Florida, a forest island is a rise in altitude of 15-30 feet that creates a drier environment with a different kind of flora. Usually the island consists of a grassy expanse loaded with slash or longleaf pine.

From the parking lot, hike west on SR 46 for 0.1 miles, and then turn left (south) on the Ocala Trail. After another 0.1 miles you will encounter a spur trail to the left that has a small signpost that reads "sinkhole." Take the spur trail. Hike for .75 miles and stop by the impressive sinkhole on the right. A rope is attached to a tree so you can swing out over the sink. Think twice, I sense disaster. Remember, in the wilderness it is YOUR responsibility not to get hurt. On the other side of the trail is the exit to Jody's Trace, where you will complete the loop and head back to your vehicle. Hike 100 feet south and you will be at Pat's Island, a gorgeous, shady expanse with tall longleaf pine.

Backpacking on the island is extraordinary. As the sun sets amid the mature pine, the western sky will explode with an orange and red palette. After the sun disappears, fog descends on the island coming from a slight hill that contains the Long cemetery.

In 1876 Reuben and Sarah Long established a homestead on Pat's Island along the Ocala Road. Boats would disembark supplies at Silver Glen Springs off of Lake George, and then wagons would haul them to Ocala. (Today the area is accessible only by foot.) The Long family grew sugar cane for a cash crop while developing a small community with a store, one-room schoolhouse and public cisterns for their water supply.

One year the Long's son Melvin adopted a fawn named Dogwood. Fifty years later, author Marjorie Kinnan Rawlings spent time at the Long's homestead and heard the story of Melvin and his fawn. She was inspired to write *The Yearling*, a Pulitzer Prize-winning novel. The novel was made into a movie starring Gregory Peck, Jane Wyman, Claude Jarman, Jr., Chill Wills and Forrest Tucker and filmed on location in 1946. Originally, Spencer Tracey had the lead role, but he found the story too corny and the "bugs and heat insufferable." After MGM invested over $50,000 in the film, Tracey got fed up and left the set in a taxicab. The first shoot was scrapped. Luckily, the filmmakers returned with a new cast and created a classic.

The Long family still holds a family reunion at Pat's Island every year.

After visiting the cemetery, hike east along the old Ocala Road, now called the Yearling Trail. After 0.5 miles turn left onto Jody's Trace. Jody was the name of the boy who adopted the fawn in Ms. Rawlings' novel. You will pass through a beautiful oak and pine forest. Watch for the cisterns on the right. When you reach the sinkhole, turn right and return to the parking lot.

Sidenote: Apparently, at the turn of the century, a friend or relative of the Long's was killed in a freak accident at a local sawmill. He was decapitated by one of the big saws. When the family buried him in the cemetery on the hill at Pat's Island, his head had somehow been misplaced. Local legends claim that: 1) a headless body stands guard at the cemetery gate during the witching hour, and 2) a head floats across the island with the evening mist. Gulp!

Hike # 16

The Yearling Trail

"Wilderness holds answers to more questions than we have yet to ask."
—Nancy Wynn Nexhall

Directions – From Ocala drive east of SR 40 for 28 miles. Turn left (north) on U.S. 19. Drive north for 7 miles and look for parking lot on left (west) side of the road.

The Yearling Trail is a 4.5-mile loop that will cover some familiar ground. Hike west for 1.5 miles through a forest of burnt sand pine skeletons, victims of a 2002 prescribed burn that reportedly went awry. Yet, note how the greenery is returning and the sand pine restoration has begun. At 1.5 miles you will pass Pat's Island and the Long cemetery again. It is just past the cemetery where this trail really starts to shine. The section from the cemetery to the Ocala Trail, and back to the sinkhole, is my favorite hike in the Ocala National Forest.

Besides being located entirely within the Juniper Prairie Wilderness, The Yearling Trail is also smack dab in the heart of the Ocala National Forest. The Ocala National Forest was established in 1908 and is the oldest national forest east of the Mississippi River. It is also the southernmost national forest in the continental United States. The Ocala has 430,447 acres and over 600 natural lakes and ponds. There are also several first magnitude springs and their runs, including Juniper, Alexander and Silver Glen.

In the area of the Yearling Trail, the Florida black bear population has its highest concentration in the state. Wild boar, whitetail deer, gray and red fox, coyote, and bobcat also roam the wilderness area. Recently, there have been discussions about reintroducing the Florida panther and eastern red wolf.

At the Long's Cemetery, continue hiking west for 0.8 miles down a gentle, picturesque slope. The slash and longleaf pine are the largest in the entire forest. You are now entering perhaps the most beautiful section on the Ocala Trail. The Ocala Trail is a 67-mile section of the Florida Trail, which traverses the state from Key West to Pensacola. There is talk of connecting the Florida Trail with the Appalachian Trail, which presently begins (or ends) on Springer Mountain in North Georgia. The addition would add over 800 miles to the 2,100-mile AP, the granddaddy of all American trails.

Turn right (north) on the Ocala Trail, and for the next 1.2 miles prepare yourself to be wowed and wowed again. As you near SR 46, watch for the signpost to the sinkhole and Pats Island. Turn right, passing the sinkhole, and then make a left (east) on the Yearling Trail and hike the 1.5 miles back to your car. Though this trail is somewhat repetitious of the Pat's Island Trail, it's well worth it to see the new sections, especially the unbelievable part from the Long's cemetery to the sinkhole trail.

In October 2004, following heavy downpours from Hurricane Ivan, three friends and I hiked The Yearling Trail. Near the intersection with the Ocala Trail, the path vanished into a newly flooded area. Since it was shorter to continue, we stubbornly pushed on through clusters of saw palmetto and followed the rim of the water while scouting the trees for the red trail markers.

"Snakes?" a friend asked.

"They're out here," I said. "Just tread lightly."

The next day in the shower I noticed 50 or 60 little red bumps on my thighs and butt that made me look like I had contacted measles or the plague. The bumps also caused an attack of itching that could ignite mental disorders.

The red marks were chiggers, or red bugs, which are a particularly nasty insect that chews its way under the skin and causes immense irritation. After a lifecycle of a week, the bug, or larvae, detaches itself from the skin and leaves an inflamed, itchy red bump. If you cover each bite with nail polish, the bug will die and hasten the healing process. Most drug stores sell a chigger medicine that is sticky and smells like nail polish.

    Later, I saw one of my friends.

    "Did you get any chigger bites?" I asked.

    He scratched his belly and sighed with relief. "So that's what these 85 red bumps are. I thought I had been experimented on by aliens."

Hike # 17

Silver Springs State Park River Trail

"What would I do if four bears came into my camp? Why, I would die of course. Literally shit myself lifeless."

—Bill Bryson

Directions – Drive east out of Ocala on SR 40 for 5 miles. Turn right (south) on SR 35 or Baseline Road. Follow signs to state park entrance and turn left (east). Drive to parking lot at the end of the road.

The River Trail in Silver Springs State Park is an easy 1.6-mile roundtrip to a splendid spot on the banks of the Silver River, or run. In Florida, a run is a short stretch of river originating from a spring and emptying into a lager body of water. For example, the Silver River, or run, flows five miles before joining the much longer Ocklawaha River. Many small runs in North Florida, including the Rainbow, Juniper and

Ichetucknee, have crystal clear water and are delightful for kayaking, canoeing, tubing, snorkeling or swimming.

The River Trail is atop an old hard-packed coquina shell road that was built when the property was privately owned. Fortunately, today the shores of the entire Silver River are in public hands.

The Silver River is the most beautiful river in the world. Please, don't take my word for it. Simply watch re-runs of the popular TV series *Sea Hunt* that ran from 1958 to 1961 and starred Lloyd Bridges. Most of the underwater scenes were filmed at Silver Springs. Or check out a midnight showing of the campy but still spooky 1954 film *The Creature From The Black Lagoon*, starring Richard Carlson, Julie Adams and Richard Denning. In the film, the Silver River and springs doubles as the Amazon River. This was one of the first movies to use top-of-the-line underwater photography and remains one of the most enjoyable monster movies of all-time. Or watch the underwater scenes in Ian Fleming's *Thunderball* and *Never Say Never*, starring Sean Connery as James Bond, or *Moonraker* with Roger Moore playing 007. If this is not enough, pick out one of the old Tarzan movies, starring Johnny Weismuller and Maureen O' Sullivan. The entire collection was filmed along the banks of the Silver River. In fact, the Silver River has sported monkeys on its shores for over seventy years. According to local legend, rhesus monkeys escaped from the Tarzan movie set and flourished, but in reality it was a tour boat operator who introduced the monkeys in the 1930s to enhance his river cruise business.

Or you could just go there, as I have many times. My wife and I love Silver River so much that we have decided, hopefully on some far distant day, to have our ashes sprinkled into the main springs.

While you enjoy life on the edge of the river, consider hiking the 0.5-mile loop trail that begins steps away from the kayak ramp. The trail loops around an overgrown expanse where the 1965 movie *Blindfold* was filmed, starring Rock Hudson and Claudia Cardinale. Unfortunately, the old cabin that was used in the movie was torn down.

My advice is to hike the River Trail only during the winter months and on a weekday. The trail normally boasts large weekend crowds.

Hike # 18

Silver Springs State Park Swamp Trail

"Wilderness is not a luxury, but a necessity of the human spirit."
—Edward Abbey

Directions – Same as the River Trail in Silver Springs State Park (Hike #17).

From the parking lot at the end of the road, walk under the River Trail arch and turn left for the Swamp Trail. I like the Swamp Trail better than the River Trail because it usually doesn't have the crowds, even on a weekend. Also, the Swamp Trail is spookier, and I'll tell you why later.

The Swamp Trail is a 2-mile roundtrip through river hammocks and cypress forests. The final 200 yards takes you on a boardwalk through a giant cypress grove above the swamp. The forests in the flood plain are at their thickest. The boardwalk leads to a small observation deck overlooking the Silver River. It's very quiet and peaceful on the deck and the view is magnificent.

Be careful of moccasin, or cottonmouth. The snakes like to curl around tree branches or skim along the surface of the water. Also, alligators are known to swim past the deck. I wouldn't swim here. Stay on the boardwalk. Besides the snakes, alligators and muck, there is a healthy growth of poison ivy.

Do not feed the monkeys. The brazen little imps have no fear and look at you as a food dispensary. One of the worst things a human being can do to wild animals is feed them. Feeding them will cause dependency on human handouts and create bad behavior on the part of the animals. They lose their natural fear of people and have no problem approaching you for a snack. I've had young alligators actually follow my boat because some thoughtless pinheads have fed them. Aggressive alligator or bear can pose a serious problem. Also, no one wants a frisky squirrel or possum to nip at your feet. Bad animals, if they become problematic or injure a human, will be destroyed. They may be moved to a less populated location, but usually they will lose their lives. Remember that the next time you toss a marshmallow to a begging wild animal. No, you're not the first one to feed them, but you could be the last.

On the deck, gaze into the crystal clear water of America's finest river. Unfortunately, the purity has become questionable because of invasive fertilizer nitrates and sewage from septic tanks. Look for otter, turtles, gar and all kinds of other fish. The river birds, including blue heron, egrets and cormorants are spectacular.

The reason I call the Swamp Trail spookier than the River Trail is because of the legend of the woman of the springs, or swamp. On misty evenings, a young beautiful woman with dark hair and pale features is rumored to rise from the mist and float above the river and swamp. Seminole legends tell of a young maiden who went to the river's edge to rendezvous with a lover she was forbidden to see. She disappeared, never to be seen again, except on misty nights. My guess is it was a bedtime story to frighten young girls who disobeyed their parents.

On the return trip to the parking lot, take a right at the first fork to explore the upland region of the state park. I can almost guarantee you will see wild boar, or pigs. Don't worry, the boar are well-behaved animals and will skeedaddle the second you approach. In March both wildflowers and shade are also plentiful.

Before leaving, visit the Seminole and Cracker villages, and the fine museum at park headquarters.

Hike # 19

Silver Springs Conservation Area

*"Between every two pines is
a doorway to a new world."*
—John Muir

Directions – From Ocala, drive east on SR 40 or Silver Springs Boulevard for 2 miles. Turn right on NE 7th Street, or Sharps Ferry Road. After driving 3 miles, look for signs and parking lot entrance on the left (north).

Silver Springs Conservation Area is a new park located just outside Ocala's city limits. Wedged between CR 35, Wal-Mart and a residential neighborhood, it's hard to believe these 330 acres southwest of the famous springs became public space. The acreage was purchased in 2005 and opened in 2010 by the Florida Forever Program, another visionary plan to protect and preserve eco-sensitive areas.

The reason the Conservation Area was acquired is to help clean up and preserve Silver Springs. The acreage is a crucial recharge area for the local aquifer that feeds the springs. As rain falls onto the landscape, it percolates down into the aquifer to filter through limestone and emerge from the spring's vents into the Silver River. The Conservation Area demonstrates the importance of maintaining acreage surrounding the springs and keeping it as pristine as possible. Fertilizers, pesticides, unregulated septic tanks and polluted runoff water are the enemy, and the farther away we can keep these pollutants the better it is for the health of Silver Springs and its river. The Conservation Area is not part of the Silver Springs State Park, yet it is crucial for its survival. This is an important issue, folks. Large-scale development and agriculture must have stringent regulation in areas surrounding the springs. The land should not be over-developed, and farms cannot continue to spread fertilizers and pesticides that will poison the aquifer. Septic tanks must be built to last.

  At the present time, a billionaire—that's right, a billionaire—has requested a permit from the St. Johns River Water Management District to pump more than 13 million gallons of water a day to grow hay for his cows on 30,000 acres just five miles north of Silver Springs. The entire city of Ocala (55,000) uses slightly less water a day. So there is no misunderstanding, this billionaire not only wants to dump fertilizer, pesticides and untold amounts of cow dung onto his 30,000 acres just north of the fragile Silver Springs, he also wants to pump millions and millions of gallons of water a day out of the aquifer at a time when the granddaddy of all Florida's springs is at a historically and dangerously low level. Talk about a definition of irresponsibility, selfishness and stupidity. Who does the thinking at the St. Johns River Water Management District? Where is the leadership on this issue? Who (head of St. Johns, Florida legislature, Florida governor) has the backbone to say, "Sorry, Mr. Billionaire, but your request for the water permit is not in the best interest of the state of Florida," and then using the voice of Jerry Seinfeld's Soup Nazi add, "No permit for you!"

But I digress...

There are two stacked loop trails for a total of 2.5 miles. Cross trails on the upper loop provide an option to add an extra mile. The soul of this trail is less than 0.5 miles from the parking lot. Take a right on Deer Track Loop and soon you will reach one of the finest oak hammocks in North Florida, with two benches and two picnic tables. It's a great place to think since no other hikers will be around to disturb you. Watch for deer, gopher tortoise and the beautiful and harmless black racer snake.

Continue hiking through the oak forest, as the sounds of CR 35 fade into the distance, and take a sharp left in order to enter the most striking section of the trail. Turkey oaks and mature longleaf pine create an emerald tunnel effect. It's a serene area, and the air is filled with pine scent.

As you circle the loop, you'll come to another bench surrounded by tall oaks and cabbage palm. Wild turkey are plentiful and there is a small sinkhole nearby. This is a trail to be hiked, and hiked again.

The preserve still appears undiscovered by the general public, even though it's also only five miles from Ocala's downtown square. After your hike, head to the square for coffee at Starbucks or dinner at Harry's Seafood Bar and Grille.

Hike # 20

Woody's Trail

"None know how often the hand of God is seen in a wilderness but them that roves it."
—Thomas Cole

Directions – From Ocala drive east on SR 40 for 6 miles. Turn left (north) on SR 314. After 12 miles, look for signs to the Ocala/Florida Trail. If you pass CR 88 or enter Salt Springs, you've gone too far. Go back and look some more. Unfortunately the signs are small. Park on the south side of SR 314 and lock your car.

This is only the second time I have you hiking on the Ocala section of the Florida Trail. There are 67 miles of this section from SR 42 to Rodman Dam. Any section you choose is scenic, especially the areas north of Lake Delancey or south of Alexander Springs.

I named this 3-mile roundtrip section "Woody's Trail" in honor of my big black Labrador, Woodstock, or Woody. It was Woody's favorite trail. Hike 1.5 miles southeast from the trailhead to a long depression on the right that is filled with mature longleaf pine. I refer to the area as the little valley. Cross to the southern slope, and set up your picnic among the pines overlooking the little valley.

Watch for deer, fox, bobcat and wild turkey, and look to the sky for hawks and bald eagle.

Once, while hiking Woody's Trail, the sky opened up and pelted the ground with a hard rain. I took out my $2.99 orange poncho and got down on one knee. Woody squeezed his ninety-five pounds under my arm, and we proceeded to wait out the shower. Thunder boomed and lightning struck nearby. A North Florida thunderstorm can be frightening and spectacular. As the storm finally began to pass, I noticed another hiker marching down the trail. He wore state-of-the-art raingear and pants, and was vigorously clicking his state-of-the-art hiking poles. When he saw me hiding under the cheap poncho, he got a smirk on his face.

He said, "You look like you need to visit Brassington's, son."

"What for?"

"Outfit yourself with some real equipment."

"I'll manage."

He noticed a tail wagging. "Who you got under there?"

I lifted the poncho and Woody poked out his head. "This is Woody."

"Hi, Woody," he said.

Woody lifted his paw and the guy shook it.

"Nice dog."

"Thanks."

"Hey, Woody," he said. "You need to leave this amateur and tag along with a real hiker."

"Funny," I said. "You're a funny guy. Hey, do those poles actually work or are they just supposed to make you look dorky?"

He left in a huff. I sat down on the poncho and opened my pack. Sadly, I discovered I had left my bottle of wine back home in the refrigerator.

"Dang," I said.

The rain took a short recess and Woody disappeared. I hoped he wasn't taking up the pole hiker's offer. Thunder continued to ripple across the sky.

I like to consider myself a spiritual being, and often claim to be a wilderness mystic. The hikes listed in this book help to confirm my belief in a higher force or power. For a brief moment, a tiny ray of sun broke out and shone on the center of the little valley. At that moment, Woody dashed between two pine trees and stopped directly in the sunshine. It was a surreal moment. The gap of light closed up almost immediately and the rain returned with a vengeance. The scene had been so stunning, I wondered if it had been a sign or omen. Perhaps the all-powerful was on the verge of revealing its existence.

I waited. Nothing happened.

On the drive home, the rain pounded harder and created a treacherous condition on the road. I slowed down and gripped the steering wheel. Visibility was low and sheets of water covered the pavement. I was still fuming about forgetting my wine. Just at that moment, I passed a weathered country Baptist church off SR 40. It had a sign out front that read, "The Lord Works In Mysterious Ways."

Nice cliché, I thought. Then I remembered my wine, and it hit me like a bolt of lightening. As the storm continued to howl, a chill ran up my spine.

Holy moly! I realized it was a blessing that I had forgotten my wine. If I had lingered, drinking wine, my drive home in the foul weather would have been much more treacherous.

Hike # 21

Pruitt Trail

*"May your search through
nature lead you to yourself."*
—K. Hymoke

Directions – From Ocala drive west on SR 200 for 12 miles. Turn right on CR 484. After driving for 6 miles, start looking for trailhead signs and turn left just past the Dunnellon airport. Parking lot is 0.5 miles on the right.

Pruitt Trail is a 10.4-mile roundtrip on the Greenway just outside the town of Dunnellon. Of course, you can hike as far as you like. I have a theory about roundtrip trails. You only have to concern yourself with the mileage going out. A 10.4-mile hike suddenly becomes only 5.2 miles. Why? Because once you've made it out, no matter how tired or sore, you will muster the strength to hike back. I always tell my hiking partners not to worry about the return trip. Whatever our condition, we are coming home.

    I'll refrain from once again ranting about the stupidity of the 1936 Cross Florida Barge Canal or praising President Nixon's visionary decision to halt construction. But the Pruitt Trail is on land that had been part of the canal route, and is now a section of the Marjorie Harris Carr Greenway. On this hike you will witness how the native habitat has swarmed over the earth to reclaim this manmade gash.

    The trail is dedicated to Mark Huffington Pruitt, son of Dr. Clayton Pruitt and Frances Pruitt, former landowners of the 8,110 acres that are now part of the Halpata Tastanaki Preserve nearby. Halpata Tastanaki was a warrior chief during the Second Seminole Indian War (1835-42). Also known as Alligator, Tastanaki played a leadership role in the defeat of Major Francis Dade and his forces. I've always wondered why the Seminole victory over Dade and 107 U.S. soldiers has never seemed to garner the attention or notoriety that other large Indian military victories have received, most notably the 1876 Sioux defeat of Lt. Col. George A. Custer at the Little Big Horn in Montana. Then I did some date comparisons, and realized that the Dade Battle on December 28, 1835 took place two months before the Battle of the Alamo in March 1836. Major Dade could not trump Col. Davey Crockett.

    Mark Pruitt was a colorful character and, more than anything else, the environmental movement is in need of colorful and charismatic characters. Henry

David Thoreau, John Muir and Edward Abbey come to mind. Pruitt, a graduate of the University of Florida's law school, was a popular and folksy local advocate. It is said he roamed the lands of the present Greenway with a parrot on his shoulder and a snake in his pocket. He touched the lives of everyone he knew with his wit, humor and curiosity. His life tragically ended September 29, 1985 in a plane crash.

I recommend hiking the old limestone road, which parallels the trail and is actually much prettier with more vistas and oak hammocks. The trail has a closed in feeling that made me feel claustrophobic, and it lacks the views.

At 0.2 miles, watch for the turnoff to the Halpata Tastanaki Preserve. In season, the preserve is a major stopover for juvenile whooping cranes as part of a federal program called Operation Migration. The operation uses manned ultra-lights, disguised as momma whooping cranes, to lead the juveniles on the southern migration path. The operation is a crucial contributor to the survival of this endangered species.

At 0.7 miles you reach a trail register under a grove of oaks. Take the short spur trail to "Stonehenge," a manmade circle of limestone boulders that form the Mark Pruitt Memorial. On my last visit, there was a pile of horse dung smack dab in the middle of Stonehenge. The horse must have been a mathematician to get it so perfectly centered. I wasn't offended. Why? Because horse riders use the trails and have been instrumental in their preservation. It demonstrates how a variety of groups and organizations, with different agendas, can create a formidable army of environmental advocates. Horse riders, hikers, backpackers, mountain bikers, kayakers and fishermen can join forces to wage battle in the environmental wars. Hunters, too. Ducks Unlimited has helped to preserve more wetlands than nearly any other environmental group.

  At 1.2 miles you'll reach an impressive stand of ancient live oaks. The first tree would take over six people holding hands in order to reach around it. Many of its limbs are thicker than most other tree trunks. They twist and arch, while creating a dense canopy that is magical, primal and spectacular.

  If you decide to push on, you'll discover some old hills on the left that were actually levees created by dirt piles during the barge canal construction days in 1936. Decent sized loblolly pines line the sides of the old levees. The pines are quite large for being only 78 years old.

  At 2.6 miles a broken-down cattle pen is visible, a remnant of the ranch and cattle days following the barge canal's decommission. I suggest a turnaround at this point, following a glass of wine.

Hike # 22

Sawgrass Island State Preserve

*"We don't stop hiking because we grow old—
we grow old because we stop hiking."*
　　　　　　　　　　　　—Finis Mitchell

Directions – I don't have a clue. I've been to Sawgrass Island four times, and each time I was arguably lost. Drive east on SR 42 out of Weirsdale. Turn right on CR 450 and start looking for signs on the left. Turn left on SE 137th Road. Good luck.

Sawgrass Island State Preserve is a 1,137-acre site located at the north end of Lake Yale in Lake County. The major feature is a 600-acre shallow marsh that is absolutely magnificent. The remaining acreage is an upland community that includes unimproved pastures, brush land, oak hammocks and longleaf pine flatwoods. Wildlife includes Sandhill crane, duck, deer, fox, gopher tortoise, alligator, pocket gopher, pine snakes and bald eagle.

    Sawgrass Island Preserve was established in 1994 to protect water quality and wildlife habitat on Lake Yale and its extensive mind-boggling marsh. The Sawgrass marsh is not only the largest natural community within the preserve, but it also serves as the largest single source of water for Lake Yale. The northern upland buffer that surrounds the marsh provides protection for the wetlands and wildlife, and also highlights the importance of bordering property to environmentally sensitive ecosystems.

    At 0.8 miles on the trail, there is a picnic table overlooking the marsh. Sit there at sunset with a glass of wine in your hand, and you'll enjoy one of the finest natural experiences in North Florida.

    The Sawgrass causeway is an easy 1.7-mile roundtrip. The trail provides awesome views of the marsh and the forested islands scattered throughout the marsh. Trust me on this one: the marsh view is more spectacular than anything in the Everglades. Watch for osprey and bald eagle soaring in the blue sky, or listen for the "rattling" of the Sandhill crane. Hike north to explore the Bent Pine Trail. There are fine views of open grasslands and oak hammocks. Check out the prickly pear cactus that at one time provided jelly for Native American tribes. Gopher tortoise love to eat the reddish fruit from the cactus. If you discover a tortoise on its back, be sure to turn him upright, please.

    Bring bug spray, even in winter.

Several historic and undisturbed Native American sites are thought to be located in the preserve, especially because of its close proximity to a food and water source. There is a wealth of Indian, Spanish and U.S. military sites in North Florida patiently waiting for ambitious archaeologists to initiate digs. So where are these professionals? Where is the funding? Much of the history of North Florida, pre-statehood, has yet to have its surface scratched. It is time for state government to exhibit some leadership on the subject. For example, in 2013 private citizens near Citra discovered artifacts from Hernando De Soto's 1539 trek from Tampa Bay to the Mississippi River. It had long been thought that De Soto's route had been 20-30 miles west of Ocala and Gainesville. Where are the University of Florida's archaeological teams?

Airboats have finally been prohibited in the preserve, yet unfortunately many of them still venture into the marsh from Lake Yale because they can. Though extremely utilitarian, there has never been a more obnoxious invention than the airboat. It can skim the water using an airplane motor and propeller. Loud does not properly describe the jarring noise that comes from an airboat. Many users operate at night, and they disturb and terrorize countless rural neighborhoods, not to mention the wildlife.

Hike # 23

Zay Prairie

"Go all the way out – come half way back."
—Heart of the Trail

Directions – Drive east out of Ocala on SR 40. After 14 miles, look for signs to Mill Dam. Turn left on FR 79 and go north for 5 miles. Zay Prairie is on the left (west) side of the road. Park off the road.

The trail is a 2.1-mile loop around a gorgeous prairie in the heart of the Ocala National Forest. There are several ponds that are wet year-round and, depending on precipitation, can be quite large. A famous landmark is the three stately Sabal palms, Florida's state tree, standing at attention in the center of the prairie. If conditions aren't too wet, you can hike out and pat them on their trunks.

Bear, skunk, deer, boar, fox, porcupine and a huge array of wading birds and raptors patrol the prairie. Two Sandhill cranes serve as hosts. I've never seen an alligator in the ponds, but to claim there are none would be foolish. Anywhere there is a bucket of water in Florida, there could be a gator.

At one time the trail loop was open to vehicles. Terrible idea. 4 x 4s with huge tires began to root and tear up the terrain, so the forest service wisely closed all road access. Unfortunately, local off-road enthusiasts have developed the habit of driving around or over barriers and making the prairie and its loop trail a playground for their monster trucks. While it's certainly impossible to control the amount of jackasses born into this world, it would be nice to provide the Forest Service with enough funding to protect the prairie and enforce laws throughout our National Forests. This is one big issue where rangers have a legitimate beef. After all, the rangers are still the front line of defense for our national wild lands. Funding cuts to the United States National Forest and Parks Service are a national disgrace.

Illegal off-roaders aside, the prairie loop is a lovely and usually lonely hike, although some parts of the trail may be sandy. On the loop, several quiet forest roads head off in different directions and invite you to explore thick forests of sand pine and live oak. Also on the loop are several open campsites for backpackers. I've camped on Zay Prairie several times and the sunrises can be magnificent. While sunsets are blocked by the oaks and pine, the colors reflecting off the ponds, prairie and sky are surreal.

At night, Zay Prairie is one of the best spots in the North Florida to check out the constellations, shooting stars and satellites, or watch the moonrise over the water. When NASA's shuttle program was up and running, I watched two shuttles blast off from Cape Canaveral into the night sky.

During one of my visits to Zay Prairie, I hiked out in the late afternoon and started a fire. Once the sun fell behind the trees, the temperature plummeted into the low 40s, which is very cold by Florida standards. I kept the fire going and sipped an adult beverage until it was dark, and then hiked out with a flashlight. Next to the second pond a couple of wild boar blocked the trail. Shining my light and yelling did no good. Finally, I flung a good-sized branch in their direction and they scampered toward the pond, grunting and snorting.

Hike # 24

Horseshoe Lake

"What is life? It is the flash of a firefly. It is the breath of a buffalo in the wintertime. It is the little shadow which runs across the grass and loses itself in the sunset."

—Blackfoot Poem

Directions – Drive east out of Ocala on SR 40 for 4 miles. Turn left (north) on CR 315. Drive 11 miles and pass through Fort McCoy. Continue driving north for 5 more miles. Turn left (west) on CR 318. Look for park signs. The turnoff is on the left (south) side of the road.

Horseshoe Lake is a diamond in the rough county park, and it sure is out in the boonies. You will want to stay clear of the park during the summer months because the swimming beach is usually filled with screeching kids. But when the months are too chilly for swimming, hardly a soul visits the park.

Horseshoe Lake was purchased through Marion County's Pennies For Parks. Using a halfpenny sales tax for a limited amount of years, Pennies For Parks scooped up land for recreational purposes and preservation. Every county in the nation should have a similar program.

Horseshoe Lake is not near anywhere, unless you want to call the hamlet of Orange Springs somewhere. The park is certainly off the radar. It has rental cabins, a picnic area with tables and grills, a swimming beach and a place to launch kayaks or canoes. The lake is a small, crystal clear spring-fed body of water that is typical of the lakes that dot the North Florida region. It even has a 1.8-mile nature trail that winds through a thick pine forest.

I suggest hiking the 1.2 miles around the lake. On the trail, you quickly fade from view of the beach area and can find shade along the southern shore. Standing at the edge of this beautiful blue lake with a wall of pine lining its rim is especially soothing to the soul. This is a place where a person can get some real thinking done.

In the winter, there is no one to collect the entrance fee. It is on the honor system. I always make certain to put my three dollars into an envelope and drop it in the box. Recently there was an interesting debate among the Marion County Commissioners, who had no role in purchasing the park. Led by the local Boss Tweed, the Commission attempted to sell the park to developers using the argument that no one uses the park during the winter. Hello! Most North Florida lakes are too cold to use during the winter months. It's a good guess Boss Tweed was friends or partners with the interested developers. Tweed claimed county tax payers should not be burdened with the cost of keeping the park open, which was a big lie since the summer fees collected covered the cost of all park maintenance. Then Tweed angrily proclaimed, "No one uses the park!" which was another fat lie. Reporters from the Ocala Star Banner went out to the park during the winter and found the gates were being locked during operating hours. Duh! If the gates are locked, it does make it difficult for people to use the park. It's also another good guess that Commissioner Tweed had something to do with the locked gates.

Government skullduggery at its finest.

Fortunately, local supporters and the Star Banner made such a fuss that the Commission dropped its plans to sell the park.

Historically, the area surrounding Horseshoe Lake had a notorious reputation for moonshining. Honest to God, there is a town nearby called Scrambletown. The town earned its name during the Prohibition years. When government agents entered the area, all the residents of Scrambletown scrambled. Several short stories by Pulitzer Prize winning author Marjorie Kinnan Rawlings document the history and characters of Scrambletown.

Hike # 25

East Grove Trail
Cross Creek

"Live in the sunshine, drink the wild air."
—Ralph Waldo Emerson

Directions – From Ocala, drive north on U.S. 301 for 26 miles to Island Grove. Turn left (west) on CR 325 and after 3 miles look for signs to the Marjorie Kinnan Rawlings State Historic House on the left.

Between Orange and Lochloosa lakes, connected by Cross Creek, is the historic home of author Marjorie Kinnan Rawlings. Her novel *The Yearling*, her memoir *Cross Creek* and dozens of her short stories are set in the surrounding region. Ms. Rawlings' rural home is a North Florida heritage site.

After divorcing from her husband Charles Rawlings, Marjorie Kinnan Rawlings of Rochester,

New York moved to a 78-acre orange grove in Cross Creek, Florida. She lived alone in a cracker-style house on the property for the duration of the Great Depression. Chastised by her editor, the legendary Maxwell Perkins, to stop trying to write romantic novels, Rawlings took a closer look at the people and stories from her rural community, and created gritty realistic tales and characters. She became fascinated by the remote wilderness and unique lives of her North Florida cracker neighbors. In 1941 she married Norton Baskin and divided her time between Cross Creek and their home at Crescent Beach, south of St. Augustine.

Park at the historic house and tour the Marjorie Kinnan Rawlings State Park. Ornamental gardens with flower varieties cultivated by Rawlings herself surround the farmhouse. Take the guided tour of the house.

Then go on a hike.

The East Grove Trail is a wide path that begins on the other side of the highway directly across from Rawlings' home. It was once the access road to a young grove of orange, tangerine and grapefruit trees, and now travels east through a large oak hammock. I've hiked this 1.3-mile trail three times and have yet to see another hiker. Most visitors to the State Park stick with the house and garden tours on the other side of the road.

The loop trail follows the old East Grove Road, hence its name. Rawlings once wrote: "Close the rusty gate and step inside the orange grove, out of the world and into the mysterious heart of another." Rawlings planted the grove in the early 1930s, but several hard freezes eventually killed off most of the trees. The crescent hammock is now regaining its original foothold and stands today as an example of the dense hammocks that once dominated North Florida. In other words, the old grove is now becoming "The Real Florida."

After your hike, drive 0.25 miles west on CR 325 and enjoy a fabulous dinner at the famous Yearling Restaurant on Cross Creek. Or turn east on CR 325 to visit the Island Grove Winery and sample a local vintage. Cheers!

Epilogue – We Have To Care

*"The idea of wilderness needs no defense,
it only needs defenders."*
—Edward Abbey

As citizens of the United States of America, we must do everything in our power, and more, to protect and defend the American landscape. We have to do it, you and me, there is nobody else.

We have to care.

"I'm a patriot of the North American continent."
—Utah Phillips

Happy Trails

"Nature's peace will flow into you
as sunshine flows into the trees."
—John Muir

Happy trails to you, until we meet again.
Happy trails to you, keep smilin' until then.
Who cares about the clouds when we're together?
Just sing a song and bring the sunny weather.
Happy trails to you, till we meet again.

(from "Happy Trails" by Dale Evans Rogers)

A Clear Midnight

This is thy hour O Soul, thy free flight into
    the wordless,
Away from books, away from art, the day
    erased, the lesson done,
Thee fully forth emerging, silent, gazing,
    pondering the themes thou lovest best,
Night, sleep, death and the stars.

Walt Whitman

Recommended Reading

1. *Desert Solitaire*, Edward Abbey

2. *The Yearling*, Marjorie Kinnan Rawlins

3. *Tourist Season*, Carl Hiassen

4. *50 Great Walks in North Florida*, Lucy Beebe Tobias

5. *The Everglades: River of Grass*, Marjory Stoneman Douglas

6. *Hiking Florida: A Guide to Florida's Greatest Hiking Adventures*, M. Timothy O'Keefe

7. *Florida State Parks: A Complete Recreation Guide*, Michael Strutin

8. *Explorer's Guide: 50 Hikes in Central Florida*, Sandra Friend

9. *Hiking The Florida Trail: 1,100 Miles, 78 Days, Two Pair of Boots*, Johnny Molloy

10. *The Monkey Wrench Gang*, Edward Abbey

Acknowledgments

I wish to express my sincere and profound appreciation for the stunningly beautiful region known as North Florida.

Thank you to my hiking buddies for the incredible adventure: Todd Carstenn, Chris Kent, Bobby Kent, Larry Larson, Elaine Springer Kent, Rob Burgess, Tom Dann, John Kerley, Lou Morrison, Bill Abbey, Howard Conrad, Craig Lipscomb, Michael Fritch, Tom Natalino, Cyndra Joi Anderson and Keith Baumann.

Special thanks to my editor Dan Barth. You are a friend and inspiration.

About the Author

G. Kent lives in the wilds of the Ocala National Forest in North Florida. He was born and raised in Los Angeles. He is also the author of *Running with Razors and Soul: A Handbook for Competitive Runners* (Bandit Press, 2013), and two novels, *Bandits on the Rim* (Tenacity Press, 2012) and *Grinners* (Bandit Press, 2014). For more information contact kentib@earthlink.net.

Front cover photo of Sunnyhill Restoration Area and back cover photo of G. Kent at the Canyons Zip Line north of Ocala by Rob Burgess.

www.ingramcontent.com/pod-product-compliance
Lightning Source LLC
Chambersburg PA
CBHW071515040426
42444CB00008B/1649